PRAISE FOR

Unspoken

A Father's Wartime Escape. A Son's Family Discovered

TOM McGRATH

Gill Books

Gill Books
Hume Avenue
Park West
Dublin 12
www.gillbooks.ie

Gill Books is an imprint of M.H. Gill and Co.

© Tom McGrath 2022

978 07171 92540

Edited by Rachel Pierce
Printed by CPI Group (UK) Ltd, Croydon, CR0 4YY

For permission to reproduce photographs, the author and publisher
gratefully acknowledge the following: © Alamy: 275, 307;
© Archivo General Militar de Guadalajara, Instituto de Historia
y Cultura Militar del Ejército de Tierra: 306; © Baker Family,
Courtesy of Virtual War Museum: 293; © General Register Office
Index of Births: 30; © International War Museum: 293; © Javier
Herrera: 305; © London Gazette, issue 36037: 269; © National
Archive, London: 207; © Shutterstock: 294; © Waterford County
Museum: 235.
The author and publisher have made every effort to trace all
copyright holders, but if any have been inadvertently overlooked
we would be pleased to make the necessary arrangement at the first
opportunity.

A CIP catalogue record for this book is available from the British
Library.

5 4 3 2 1

CONTENTS

PART TWO
MY STORY

A SPECIAL ACKNOWLEDGEMENT

Ever since the discoveries I have made about my family came to light, I had it in the back of my mind to put pen to paper in order to capture and preserve them. What had been holding me back from writing was the feeling that I had insufficient material to compile a comprehensive account. I had travelled to London to obtain documentary evidence from the National Archives, which included various interviews my father had with MI5, MI6 and the American equivalent after his escape. I was also given a short essay about my father's escape, which was written by his sister-in-law years after his return. These gave a snapshot of his experiences. But, apart from his account and the essay, I knew very little else about my father's life.

The reason I finally did put pen to paper was the encouragement from my son, Eric, and his wife, Anna. I found that what had been swirling around in my head was only waiting on tap, and the words flowed effortlessly. Eric and Anna were heroic. They offered to be my collaborators, even though, at the time, they were living and working in Melbourne and had just had a baby, Luca – my first grandson. Despite their busy schedules, we worked out a system to chip away at this together from opposite ends of the world. They encouraged me, made suggestions, helped with formatting and structuring the book, and strove to get the very best out of me to make what I had written the best it could possibly be.

Anna's passion for the story and dedication to capture it in a compelling manner was particularly inspiring to me. The same goes for Eric's meticulous approach and enthusiastic drive. It was especially rewarding to have Eric accompany me to several of the places as we followed my parents' footsteps. They were memorable days that we will both cherish for ever.

Without a doubt, the writing of this book has been one of the most rewarding experiences of my life. It has filled a void and fulfilled a lifetime of searching for answers about who I am and where I come from, and it has helped to bring me even closer to my parents and to get to know them better than when they were alive. Indeed, my own children, who never met them, have grown to appreciate who their grandparents were. Both of my parents found themselves in entirely separate, terrible circumstances. Both reached deep into their inner beings to fight and ultimately to overcome these hardships. Their great-grandchildren need to be told of their courage. Thank you to Eric and Anna for helping me to do this.

PROLOGUE:
LISTENING TO THE SILENCE

Throughout my childhood, there were many odd silences and matters unspoken. I never noticed any of it. As a young child you accept what you are wholeheartedly, particularly if you are surrounded by as much love and happiness as I was. It was not until years later that I realised my upbringing was different from that of my peers. Sadness and sorrow arrived only when my parents died, when I was in my teens. Now, though, I feel a different sadness and heartbreak having discovered the things I have discovered, which have led me to understand the pain and suffering my parents endured in their lives. What I would give to embrace them both now.

This book started out as a tribute to my father, whom I loved dearly, for his courageous feats during the Second World War. It was something about which he always remained silent. He never talked about that part of his life, and it appears he told only a few close family members about his war journey. I have gathered up here all those remembered glimpses into his incredible war experiences.

For over two years, I dedicated myself to carrying out extensive research on all aspects of my father's story. I read voraciously all the publications and books I could find relating to the British Expeditionary Force, the Maginot Line, Stalag XXA, the Second World War and the Resistance. In many ways, this was a delight because ever since childhood I have been fascinated by anything to do with the Second World War and with heroic escapes. I also spoke with people who knew my parents and anyone who might be able to shed some light on my family history. Some of these people knew them quite well and were able to share wonderful insights.

The big break came when I discovered an account, dictated by my father as part of his debriefing, in the National Archives in London. There, I read for the first time my father's own words and descriptions of his war experiences. It opened a conversation with my father that I am still engaged in to this day. It allowed me to finally hear the things he never said to me.

Unexpectedly, while researching this book I also discovered new, hidden information about my mother that showed what a brave woman she was. I also loved her deeply and I hope that the words I have written will provide her with the long overdue vindication she deserves.

The following is a work of non-fiction inasmuch as I tell my own story and the surprising truths that I uncovered in my parents' stories. In trying to piece together the experiences of my parents, I gathered as much evidence as I could and then used fiction in an attempt to understand the unspoken parts of their lives. I wanted to imagine the blanks, to try to conjure up what they must have gone through, to try to walk in their shoes during the most challenging parts of their lives. To imagine is to begin to understand; that is the basis of this account. Undoubtedly, some things didn't happen in exactly the way I have written them. There were many dots to connect. But without trying to connect them, how else could I have made sense of it all?

What I have set out to do is to leave an account of a time in history that placed ordinary people, through no fault of their own, in cruel and dangerous situations. The unusual nature of this story – a mix of fact and fiction – allows me to explore their lives in detail and also the times in which they lived.

So much of our lives are unspoken. If we don't speak into those silences, others will. I am happy to be the one to tell the stories of my mother and father – as they are remembered, recorded and imagined.

PART ONE

MY FATHER'S STORY

BASED ON THE RECORDED ACCOUNT OF HIS WAR
EXPERIENCES AND ESCAPE, HELD AT THE NATIONAL
ARCHIVES, LONDON, AND ON HIS CONVERSATIONS WITH
FAMILY MEMBERS AFTER THE WAR YEARS

The father I knew.

The father I discovered.

1.

PORTLAW TO ALDERSHOT
1904-1939

My name is Tommy. I was born on 17 January 1904, the seventh of thirteen children, two of whom died in infancy. My father and mother had a large family and, though they were not wealthy, they did their best to provide for all of us with great love and affection. Originally, we lived in a small house on George's Street in the village of Portlaw, which is twelve miles from Waterford City in the south of Ireland. By small, I mean a little one-storey house that was shared with my father and mother and my five brothers and five sisters. In later years, when my father was promoted to head forester in the Curraghmore Estate, my family moved to a larger house in Coolfin, on the outskirts of the village.

We had a tough life, yet it was vibrant and challenging. The central square in the town had only horses and carts traversing it, with some hitched to the posts outside the small family-run shops. The place was often bustling with farmers and tradesmen, little old ladies in shawls, old men in caps with clay pipes dangling from their moist lips, some walking on the dusty ground, others gathered in small groups for a hearty chat. The inside of the local public house, Harney's, with its dark and smoke-filled bar, yellow walls and sawdust-covered floor, was the focal point of the town's social universe.

We endured the bitter cold during the winter months. All we had was a small turf fire in the kitchen to heat our humble dwelling. The cramped living conditions, the screams, the cries and the laughter of my brothers and sisters bellowing forth from the tiny house on George's Street – that was home.

There were many days of wonderment and joy. Days spent playing in the open fields and splashing about in the crystal-clear waters of the nearby lakes and the Clodiagh River, all the while wrapped in the security and comfort of companionship, feisty rivalry and a feeling of belonging. The excitement and challenges encountered on the local hurling pitches, when either playing for or cheering on the local team, cemented our shared sense of camaraderie. And then the awkward transition from adolescent to man, taking on the mantle of responsibility, whether it was chopping wood in the forest, hauling sacks in the mill or curing skins in the tannery.

In my late teens I worked in the forest on the Curraghmore Estate of Lord Waterford. I met a local girl called Mary Fowler in the village and we started courting. She and I got married in the Catholic church in Portlaw on 4 May 1927. For a while, I continued to work in the forest while Mary did house-keeping for two elderly sisters in a large house just outside the village. Although wages were low, we lived comfortably. Nevertheless, something within me made me restless and sparked a desire to seek a life elsewhere.

One day in 1930, I saw an advertisement in the local Waterford newspaper, *The Munster Express*. A wealthy family in Surrey, England, was looking to employ a gardener and a housekeeper. We nervously sent off our application and, some weeks later, received word that we had been successful and that we could start the following week.

We sold whatever furniture we owned and packed the few personal belongings we had into a little old suitcase. Having said our goodbyes to our families and friends, Mary and I boarded the bus that would take us to the railway station in Waterford. From there, the three-hour journey found us alighting onto the platform at Kingsbridge Station in Dublin.

It was damp and cold as we made our way on foot to the city centre from where we would take a tram to bring us to the harbour at Dún Laoghaire to board the boat to England.

'Don't cry, Mary,' I said putting my arms around her to comfort her. 'We'll be alright, you'll see. Things will be grand.'

We were both numb but had hardly even noticed the chill. It was fear of the unknown that had frozen us stone-cold. We were young, innocent and naive to the ways of the world. Neither of us had ever set foot outside our own local community and yet we were also hugely excited to be setting off on this journey to the big lights and a whole new world.

Having travelled all night by boat and train, we finally arrived at London's Euston Station. From there, we took a bus to our new employer's residence in Leatherhead, Surrey. During the journey, we were mesmerised by the sounds and sights of the biggest place we had ever seen. There were cars, buses and trams of every variety, and buildings so big that we could not grasp how they could stay up, nor imagine how they possibly could have been constructed. We were two lost souls in a strange new environment. We knew no one and could barely understand a word through the heavy local accents.

At the house of Dr Graham Maxwell and his wife, Dorothy, a butler opened the door and asked us to step into the parlour. A little while later, the doctor presented himself, shook our hands and told us we were very welcome.

We were accommodated in a small flat, 23 Kingscroft Road, not far from the Maxwells' home. Our employers treated us very well. Mary looked after the housekeeping and cooking while I tended to the extensive gardens encircling the premises. About a year after our employment commenced, Dr Maxwell told me that he wanted to send me on a course to learn how to be a car mechanic. He also said that he wanted me to learn to drive because I would be his new chauffeur when Richard, his current driver, retired.

Our jobs were demanding, and life was not easy, but overall we were happy. Of course, there was always the constant sorrow in our hearts of missing our families and friends back home, but we had each other and that was all we needed.

———

Throughout 1939, there had been a lot of talk and newspaper coverage of what was happening in Germany. This was brought to a head when Germany invaded Poland on 1 September 1939 and, soon after, war was declared by France and Britain in response.

Early one morning, while I was at the sink drying my face after shaving, I spotted the outline of the postman through the lace curtains above the mirror. He was leaning his bicycle against the garden gate. He knocked on the door and handed me a letter. From the emblem on the envelope, I immediately knew what it was. It was a notice from the Ministry of Defence instructing me to report to Aldershot Garrison for training. I was being conscripted into the British Army.

Out in the kitchen, Mary and I locked eyes. My mind was racing.

'Oh! Tommy, they'll send you to fight.' As tears rolled down her cheeks, she whispered, 'I'll never see you again. What am I going to do here? I'll never survive on my own.'

'It'll be fine,' I said. 'Sure, I hear that nothing will come of it, and this is all just a precaution.'

'Can we not go home? They can't make you join up.'

'That's not the answer, Mary. You have to understand that once I've received this letter, I have no choice.'

—————

It was little over an hour by train from Leatherhead to Aldershot, although the journey seemed to take for ever. The dank carriages were bursting at the seams, mostly full of young men engaged in nervous banter, knowing that they were embarking on a journey, the destination and duration of which they could not control.

When we reached Aldershot, I joined with the mass of other men who were lining up to gain entry to the barracks. I found myself in the midst of a mob of bodies, which seemed to pull me towards the gates. I looked around at the faces of men who had already been hardened by the realities of life through hard work and toil, and faces of those who were still just boys, naive and innocent, nonchalantly chatting with one another. As we approached the registration desk, we were asked to provide our personal details: name, address, next of kin and religion.

'Right, McGrath, off you go. Follow that sign and queue up for your medical. Then report back here for your kit.'

'Sir, would it be possible for me to be assigned to the Royal Irish Regiment? My father and eldest brother fought in the Great War with that regiment, and my father was held as a prisoner of war in Limburg in Germany.'

'Now look here, Paddy, you're in the British Army now. You'll do as you're told, when you're told. Understand?'

'Yes sir, but –'

'No "but"s! Fuck off down to the medic. Now!'

The medical examination was basic. The doctor checked that I was in a general state of good health, had sufficiently good eyesight and did not have flat feet. Then I was told to report back to the gate at the main entrance and join the queue to be given my uniform, boots and weapons, which consisted of a Lee-Enfield rifle with bayonet and an Enfield revolver. We were also given a gas mask, underwear, a towel, a razor and a bar of soap.

Later that evening I was assigned to my billet, which was in a dormitory with twenty or so bunk beds. A man was already sitting on the bunk beside mine. 'I'm Frank,' he bellowed, as he thrust forth his massive hand for me to shake. I could tell he was from Yorkshire by his accent.

'Hello,' I said, 'I'm Tommy.'

'You're Irish!'

'Yes, but I've been working in England now for a number of years. I was conscripted and told to come here.'

'Bet you're sorry that you left the old sod, eh?'

'It's safe to say that this wasn't in our plans when we came, but, really, England has been good to me and my wife. It has given us a good living and, sure, everyone is saying that there'll be no war. That it's only all talk and bluff from the Germans.'

From the far side of the room, a short, stocky soldier called out, 'Not sure we bleedin' want your help, Paddy.'

I could sense the atmosphere change.

'I had no choice; I was told to be here.'

'Well, I for one don't want you. So, my little ploughboy friend, all I'm saying is watch your back, if you know what I mean,' my aggressor snarled through tobacco-stained teeth.

Later that night, when we were having supper in the general mess, I was approached by another Irishman. Having introduced himself as Jim Creagan, he said, 'I overheard that conversation earlier in the billet. Keep your eye on that little bollocks. His name is Ronnie. They tell me he has a reputation for being a tough guy who tries to make life difficult for fellows he doesn't like. Apparently, he's from London's East End and grew up tough.'

'I don't know what the hell I ever did to him.'

Jim just shrugged and said, 'Don't let him get to you, boy.'

As it turned out, Jim and I had a lot in common. We were both Irish emigrants who had come to England to find work. He had relations in Waterford and knew a lot of the places I talked about. I was glad to have found someone I could talk to and trust. In time, Jim and I developed a strong friendship which helped us enormously with the trials and horrors we were to face.

At 6 a.m. the next morning, we were woken by the loud sound of the reveille being trumpeted throughout the barracks. Its shrill pitch pierced the fresh morning air. Within thirty seconds, Sergeant Major Terence Strawbridge was stomping through the dormitory, bellowing orders for everyone to jump out and stand to attention. 'Well, good morning, my little darlings, and welcome to Aldershot. This is now your home for the next few months. This is where you will eat, drink, shit, fart and vomit until you earn the right to call yourselves soldiers. This is the place that you enter as boys and walk out as men – that is, if you survive. Do you under-stand me?'

'Yes, sir!'

'I can't hear you.'

'YES, SIR!'

'I still can't fucking well hear you. DO YOU UNDER-STAND ME?'

'*YES, SIR!*'

'You'll be glad to hear that every one of you has been assigned to the 51st Highland Division, a division typically filled with our Scottish brothers up north. But even though the bulk of you are not Scots, you'll be proud to become part of this infantry regiment, which carries such an enormously heroic pedigree and a gallant history of battles won. But I warn you, we have very high standards and I expect no less from every last one of you. Anybody who dithers, falls or fails to give me one hundred per cent will be put on half-rations for a week and will have me to reckon with.

'Normal training for infantry recruits is two years, but since we don't know what to expect from the Jerries, we must prepare you as best we can within a matter of months so as to be ready if they do make a move. Unfortunately for you, my little dears, that is not such good news. You'll be expected to work hard and not complain. You'll receive basic training on armaments, map-reading, drill, physical engagement and overall discipline. When I say jump, you'll jump. You will not question an order. From now on, you'll think like soldiers, you'll behave like soldiers and, until this conflict is over, there is no you, only your regiment. Are we clear?'

'Yes, sir!'

Days led into weeks and weeks turned into months. We were put through a gruelling regime of training, which seemed to border on torture, yet, somehow, we slowly felt ourselves grow. Our bodies became leaner, fitter and more agile. I had played hurling and football back home, but I was now finding muscles in parts of me that I never knew existed.

We were made to polish our boots until you could see yourself in them. Our trousers and kits were ironed to perfection so that the crease was razor-sharp, and the brass buttons on our uniforms glistened.

The day we were told to pick up our rifles, I was amazed at how heavy they were. Yet, after three months of daily contact, it was as if they were part of our uniform. But what shocked me most of all during our training was being shown how to use a bayonet by the sergeant major.

'Now, me laddies, I will give the order to affix bayonets. When I do, you will each attach your piece to the top of your rifle just as you were taught. You will do so in unison, and when they are attached, you will stand to attention until I give further orders.

'When I order you to attack, you will charge forth towards the hanging sandbags. Only, in your minds, they're not really sandbags. They're Jerries. And you'll drive the spearhead in deep under the ribs with all your strength and twist it as if your lives depended on it. Remember, the day will come when it will be for real, and it will be either you or him who will survive. The choice is yours. Learn to do it right now and you just might come out on top.'

I felt a knot in my stomach at the thought of what the sergeant major was saying. I could never imagine committing such an act upon another human being. When it came my turn to charge, I imagined I was running against a haystack in the field at the back of our house in Portlaw. It made it easy to do, and the sergeant major seemed pleased. I wonder did he ever suspect what was in my mind. Nor did he utter a word when I tripped on my run and fell into a pool of mud. I often asked myself if he had actually seen, all the way down the line, that it was Ronnie who had put out his foot just as I began to charge.

Towards the end of December, we all assembled in the large mess hall and were addressed by Colonel Patterson. An air of apprehension filled the room.

'Gentlemen, as you know, Hitler has no respect for treaties, or for anything else really for that matter. He has invaded Czechoslovakia, Austria and now Poland. Britain had pledged to support Poland in such an event and has, as a result, now formally declared war on Germany. We do not believe that Hitler will stop at what he has plundered thus far. Therefore, a decision has been taken to set up a defence along the France–Belgium border to support our French allies in preventing any further incursions. You are to be assigned to the British Expeditionary Force, which will commence disembarking for France beginning at 0600 hours tomorrow. I wish you all good luck and pray that this will all be over soon.'

That night, in our bunks, we nervously chatted among ourselves. 'You know that if they do invade, we'll be obliterated, don't you?' Frank's question cast a silence over the room.

'What d'you, mean, Yorkie?' Ronnie asked.

'I mean that while we were eating bread and jam, the Jerries were busy building up their army, navy and air force.'

'So much for the Treaty of Versailles! That bastard Hitler doesn't give a rat's ass for treaties – as we have seen time and time again,' retorted Jim, my Irish pal.

'Bollocks! Have you not seen that our kits, from our uniforms down to our weapons, are the same as those our fathers used in the Great War? We'll be no match for Hitler's boys if they decide to invade, which they will,' Frank replied.

'We'll just have to rely on the likes of our Paddy friend here, or his pillock family back in the bogs, soaking in whiskey, who might dig us up a few potatoes in the French fields to throw at the Jerries.' Ronnie sniggered.

'Oh, give it a break, Ronnie. It's getting tedious!' said Jim. Shortly after, the lights were turned off and I lay on my back and gazed into darkness, thinking about what might be ahead.

———

In the dead of night, I was awoken by the sound of muffled noise coming from somewhere close by. I opened my eyes but did not move. The noise continued, ever so faintly. I sensed that it had to be some disturbance close to my bunk, which meant that it was one of two things: either Frank going through his kit, or someone was rummaging through mine.

My eyes adjusted and I could make out the outline of whoever it was who had woken me. Immediately I saw that he had too small a frame to be Frank. With that, I leapt from my bunk and, with an almighty thrust, grabbed Ronnie by the shirt. I could see that he had my bag open.

'What the hell do you think you're doing? That's my kit,' I yelled.

'No, no, nothing. I made a mistake, that's all. Got confused,

I guess, ya know,' gulped Ronnie.

'I've had it with you, Ronnie! Ever since the day I arrived here, you've done nothing but cause me problems. Well, I'm not taking it anymore.' Gripping him by the collar, I lifted him a foot off the ground and pinned him to the wall. Keeping my voice low and maintaining composure, I left him in no doubt that he would regret pulling any similar tricks with me in future.

'Ah, c'mon, lad, I meant no harm. I just got mixed up, that's all.'

'Oh, yes, confused, mixed up, is it? Let me just warn you, *lad*, keep away from me in future, do you understand?'

'Sure, okay!' he gasped as I let him down.

I returned to my bunk. There was a chilled atmosphere. My muscles were tingling with frustration. *This can't go on*, I thought to myself. *This fella is a bastard, and I'm not taking any more of it.* My mind was torn. Nobody knew what was behind Ronnie's swagger. Sure, he liked to portray an image of bravado, but I wondered how he would manage when the time came to face the Jerries. Someone at the back started singing '*Pack up your troubles in your old kit bag ...*' and before long the atmosphere changed and there was boisterous harmony from all with '*and smile, smile, smile!*'

2.

LE HAVRE
JANUARY 1940

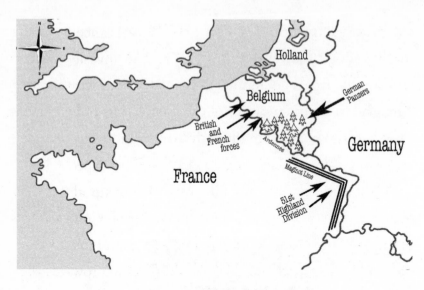

Western Europe, 1940.

The vomit swished to and fro against the ship's cold, damp walls. Each time the bow of the boat rose with the waves, the reeking swill would slink back towards the stern, only to gush forth again when the next wave was hit. The toilets were overflowing with a mucousy slime. Up on deck, ashen-faced men were doubled over the side rails in anguish, many having never set foot aboard a ship before. The weather was horrendous. A gale force wind was toying with our vessel, which was being thrust from side to side and bobbing incessantly over the white crests of the black waves. We tried our best to cling to the rails to stop ourselves being propelled overboard. Our uniforms were drenched in vomit and sea spray.

We had set sail from Southampton early that morning, having been given our orders that we were to join up with the British Expeditionary Force (BEF) in France to assist the French Army in preventing a German invasion. After crossing the English Channel in such atrocious weather, we were glad to see the rooftops of the French port of Le Havre, where we disembarked in the early afternoon. It was freezing and damp. No one had warned us of what to expect.

Orders were given for all units to line up along the quayside. Major-General Victor Fortune, the Commander of the 51st Highland Division, addressed us and told us that we would commence our advance that evening towards the Belgian border, where we were to meet our French allies, and from there advance into Belgium. Along the way, we took up positions in set locations, where we were deployed in digging anti-tank ditches and trenches in case they were required at a later stage.

It was dusk when we set off on our march east. The ground was frozen, which hampered our progress. Late that evening, we came upon a small village that seemed deserted. Some of us decided to explore the adjoining farmhouses in search of food and hay to afford a night's comfort. Later, as we lay in an empty barn, all was quiet. The village and surrounding farms had been evacuated by their populace, leaving valuable possessions behind. God knows where the poor souls had fled to.

One of our lads, Harry Mowatt, looked around and said, 'This ain't so bad. Sure, if things turn out as some say they will, and just suppose that Jerry has no interest in us, I mean, we can happily play a supporting act to the Frenchies all day long – right?'

'Oh, for fuck's sake, Harry,' Ronnie said, 'don't you bloody well know that Hitler doesn't care about borders, treaties or whatever the fuck any government says? If he wants something, he'll go for it – and the lot of us better start praying that he doesn't because with the load of shit that they've given us as excuses for weapons, he'll stomp all over us with his jackboots.'

'But Ronnie,' said Harry, 'we're here in numbers to prevent that. And sure, we have the RAF boys watching over us. Here, have a fag, relax.'

'I think Harry is right,' I said. 'We are where we are, and we have to make the most of it. Who knows, maybe when Jerry sees that we are serious about standing up to him, he'll say he has had enough.'

We chatted a while longer before settling in for the night. As silence descended in the barn, the hoot of owls could be heard in the distance, while all around me I heard the fluttering of breathing from my companions. I began to think of Mary back home in Leatherhead, her lithe body under a sheet and a blanket, her soft skin against a pillow. She would be missing me and wondering where I was. And my poor mother and father. They were so worried when I wrote to tell them that I had been conscripted. Although Daddy hardly ever spoke about it, and during the times that he did I could see it pained him, he had told me of the horrors he had witnessed in the Great War and of the suffering he had had to endure when he was captured and thrown into a prisoner-of-war camp in Limburg, Germany. The poor man had been shot in battle and had even had two fingers amputated without anaesthetic. Apparently, he had never been the same again. My brothers and sisters, who had no idea of where in the world I was, would be wondering if I was even alive. I prayed for them all. I prayed for Mary, and I prayed that everything would be over soon, and we could all go back to our lives as before. But deep down I knew that that was not going to happen any time soon. We had been trained to fight an enemy, an enemy on a rampage, who was unlikely to stop now.

Over the next ten days, we marched on through thick mud, one squelching step after another, as soaked feet struggled to release heavy, sodden boots from the clinging soil. Finally, we were told that we would set up a more long-term base in the town of Béthune, twenty miles from the Belgian border.

Within a matter of weeks, we settled into a relaxed way of life. It came to be referred to as 'the phoney war' because both sides seemed to be content with the inactivity – although many of us did speculate that the Germans were using this time to reinforce before making their attack.

Yes, we still had our training exercises and ditch-digging, but in the evenings we could visit the local hostelries and bars, where copious quantities of French beer and wine were consumed. There were card games and brawls, singsongs and fist-fights. Some of the more adventurous would wander into Lille to chance their luck with the local lassies. At times we wondered if there was going to be a war at all.

———

In late April, word spread that we were being mobilised and moved to the Saar region to coordinate a defensive back-up with French forces. On 22 April, we were detached to the Maginot Line. There was a mixture of fear and excitement among the men. Up to that point, nobody believed there would be an actual invasion. Now, however, it seemed inevitable.

Allied forces relied on the Maginot Line and the supposedly impassable Ardennes Forest to defend the French border against invading German forces. In less than a week, having travelled on foot and by train, we arrived at our destination. We were overwhelmed by the size of the fortresses that combined to make up the Maginot Line. We were told it stretched for hundreds of miles. It seemed impenetrable.

Over the following days we began the laborious task of digging trenches and command posts. By now we had heard that the enemy was only a few hundred yards away on the other side of the stream. Despite this, we managed to set up camouflaged positions that were connected by telephone lines. We were told that our mission was to gather intelligence about German movements and to establish the strength of their numbers. We were also to ascertain if there was an army build-up in force in preparation for an attack.

It didn't take us long to settle into our dugouts interspersed between the beech trees, from where we kept watch, ate and slept each day and night. It also did not take long for us to realise that the phoney war wasn't that phoney after all.

Night after night, a number of men from our unit would be picked to go out on patrol to garner as much information as possible. On occasion, there would be engagement with enemy fire. The first time I was ordered on patrol I was to accompany Billy Hamilton, Johnnie Ringrose and Sergeant Roy Murray. Billy was a young man who told me that before the war he had worked as a shop's clerk in Bromley. He looked no more than sixteen or seventeen. Johnnie was older, in his late twenties, and he had been a baker in Manchester before the war. Having blackened our faces and geared up, we proceeded out of our dugout and hunched in a crawl towards no-man's-land. Finding some gorse bushes to cover us, we straightened up and started to walk along the edge of the stream.

'What on earth brought you here, son?' I asked Billy.

'I volunteered.'

'Why would you do that? You're only a young lad.'

'I dunno,' Billy replied thoughtfully. 'I guess I wanted a taste of something more adventurous than sitting behind a cashier's till all day. And besides, this won't be for long. We all know that.'

'How old are you, lad?'

'I told the recruiting officer my real age, sixteen. He said I was too young to join up. But when he saw the look on my face, he winked and told me to go out and come back in and say that I was eighteen,' Billy chirped with a smile of satisfaction.

'And you, Johnnie, what got you here?'

'I was conscripted, had no choice really. I hate it, I hate it all! This marching, digging, marching, digging, digging, marching – I've had enough of it. And now to be thrown out with this shite on our faces to actually go looking for Jerries is horrible. I can't wait for this to end, whatever way it ends!'

'Ah, come on, man, it's not that bad,' interjected Sergeant Murray with the maturity gained from years of army life as a regular. 'Look at what our fathers went through on the Somme. I'd like to think this is a cakewalk in comparison, don't you agree, Tommy?'

'My father told me what they went through in that hell-hole,' I said. 'I would wish it on no one. The way I see it is, we have a job to do, and we have no choice in the matter, so we may as well do a good job once we're at it.'

'Sure, we have no option, lad. We have to fight the fascist fuckers, or we'll all end up speaking bloody German,' Sergeant Murray said impatiently. 'Anyway, time to move up and on. Stay close! Alright, lads?'

As we progressed along the rugged terrain, we heard a murmur of distant sounds. The sergeant ordered us to drop to our bellies and crawl ever so gently forward and upward to the lip of a ridge above the stream. There, we could see a group of ten or twelve Jerries huddled around a small camp-fire with telephone cable equipment strewn around them. In the heat of the moment, on seeing the enemy, Johnnie began to get up and, in the course of cocking his rifle, was firmly brought back to ground by Sergeant Murray, who grabbed his ankles and tripped him.

'Do you want to get us killed, you idiot?' he hissed. 'You, McGrath, take Hamilton and cut to the side. Await my order if we have to open fire. Understood?'

'Understood!' I replied nervously. We were tasked with getting a fuller picture of the group. Did it consist of only this dozen men or were there more positioned out of view? Hamilton and I crawled as silently as we could down the ridge. We crossed the stream, which again gave us a good view of the Jerries, who seemed to be chatting and generally relaxing after, no doubt, a hard day laying telephone cables from one communication centre to the next.

'Tommy, look, do you see that?' Billy whispered.

'What?'

'The radio set. If I sneak up behind them, I know I can bag it. It'll be useful to listen to what the Jerries are saying, don't you think?'

'I think you just better stay where you are and wait for the sergeant's orders.'

But the impetuous eagerness of youth meant that nothing was to stop young Billy from doing what he thought was his bit for the Crown. Despite my frantically whispered protests, I watched as he belly-crawled two hundred feet towards a clump of trees halfway between our location and the German camp-fire. To his horror, Sergeant Murray could also see what was happening. Unfortunately, so too could Johnnie Ringrose.

Whether out of tense nerves, panic or just mere stupidity, Johnnie rose to his feet and raised his rifle. As he did, a sharp cracking sound pierced the night and Johnnie Ringrose was no more. Half his head was torn off by the sheer force of a sniper's bullet that hit him before he'd had a chance to fire a single round.

Chaos erupted in the German camp. Murray and I opened fire, but we knew that we were outnumbered. We had to retreat, and fast. Just then, I saw young Billy make a run for the radio, but he was brought down when a bullet hit him in the shoulder. I shouted to Murray to cover me and, as he began firing, I sprinted in a hunkered movement and rolled to the ground beside young Billy.

'How are you, lad?' I asked breathlessly. Billy was moaning in agony, biting on his wrist to stop himself from screaming. But from what I could see, none of his vital organs had been hit and, even though he was bleeding profusely, I was sure that he could move enough to help me get him out of there.

Fortunately, Sergeant Murray had had the foresight to bring a Bren submachine gun, which he used enthusiastically, providing sufficient cover for me to get Billy to his feet and put his arm around my shoulder as I zig-zagged back to the ridge. Sergeant Murray joined me and supported Billy on his other side. With sufficient protection from the overhanging hedges, we made our way back to our base.

That night I could hardly sleep. It was the first time I had seen someone die. As much as I fought to repel it, I kept seeing Johnnie's head being torn apart. I wanted to scream with the torment that the image was causing me.

Thankfully, Sergeant Murray brought word from the medics that young Billy would be okay. His collarbone had been shattered, but he would live. 'Good work there last night, McGrath. That was a brave thing you did. You saved his life, but you almost got yourself clipped in doing so.'

'I didn't give it too much thought, to be honest, Sarge. It seemed the only thing to do, and I'm glad that I did it. But I feel so bad for Johnnie.'

'Don't! That fucker nearly got us all killed. I warned him. I told him to lie low and wait but, like so many cock-a-hoop heroes, he had to do it his way. Well, that's not how this works. You do as you're ordered and if you do so, you just might make it through this war and live to tell the tale. But that poor bastard wouldn't do that, and look where he is now.'

'I know, Sarge, you're right, but it's still so sad. Such a waste!'

In the days that followed, other patrols had their skirmishes, giving rise to further casualties. Aerial attacks by the Germans became more frequent. It seemed as if they were strategically weakening our defences in preparation for an inevitable invasion. It was interesting to observe how invariably and consistently each man's primal survival instinct was aroused when a Messerschmitt was heard approaching. Every man would go down as far as possible in the dugout hole. Most of the time the bombs missed, but at other times they didn't.

———

In mid-May, we were told that we would be retreating northwards by train to Rouen. On the morning that we were to leave, Colonel Patterson asked to see me.

'At ease, Private. As a conscript, you seem to be getting on well. I have heard good reports about you, and Sergeant

Murray filed a report to say that you saved a man's life in the field. You have shown respect and discipline and you seem to get on well with the rest of the men. McGrath, we think that you are an asset to the division, and you have bright prospects for the future. I am pleased to inform you of your promotion to corporal, effective immediately.'

'Thank you, sir.'

'Alright, dismissed!'

That evening there was lots of cheering and blackguarding, with me at the centre of it all. Overall, my friends were pleased with my promotion.

'Well, what d'ya know, will ya look at General Paddy Potato Face, isn't he a pretty sight?'

'Oh Ronnie, would you ever shut the fuck up!' shouted Frank. 'Hey, Tommy, why don't you just order the little sod to piss off.'

I smiled and thought to myself that I wasn't the only person that was being annoyed by Mr Ronnie.

'Nah! I'll wait till they make me colonel, then I'll really have him worried!'

As we settled down for what was to be our last night in the trench, we all wondered what lay ahead.

3.

SAINT-VALERY-EN-CAUX
JUNE 1940

In early June, we reached the River Somme near Abbeville. We were exhausted and confused. We had been told that we were heading for the front to assist the French forces in confronting the German invaders, yet our allies seemed in disarray, with some even moving in the opposite direction. We also later discovered that the rest of the BEF was on an entirely different course at this time. While we were on our way to engage with the enemy, the rest were steadily retreating towards Dunkirk, to be rescued by the Royal Navy and a flotilla of civilian boats manned by volunteers. At that time, we were cut off from them and had no idea of this development. The elation they must have felt at their rescue was a far cry from what we were enduring in a not-too-distant field.

During all this, the hardest thing for us to stomach was not the battle but the anticipation of what was to come. Our imaginations would run riot, envisaging all sorts of atrocities that would befall us. Unfortunately for many, some of these nightmares would prove prophetic. We were ordered to set up our position to prepare for the impending enemy engagement. Not many eyelids stayed shut on that long and agonising night.

At dawn on 4 June, we were ordered to prepare to attack the enemy in support of a fleet of French tanks as they advanced towards the German lines just over the river. Sergeant Major Strawbridge told us to follow close behind the advancing convoy. Fixing the bayonet to my rifle, as we had been instructed to do, made me feel sick to my stomach. This instruction was a clear sign that we could expect hand-to-hand combat.

As we set off, I looked around me. Everything was shrouded in a dark mist. I could see the apprehension in the eyes of my comrades as we slowly marched forward. I could sense the tension tightening their jaws as they struggled to moisten their tongues. We were parched with trepidation. The snarling roar of the tanks' engines as they forged a pattern of tracks in the light mud sounded like thunder in our ears. We trooped along behind the trundling tanks. And then it began.

All hell broke loose once we approached enemy lines. Mortars were dropped all around us. The armour of the French tanks was pierced by the bombardment of the German artillery. Little dots on the horizon soon became hundreds of enemy soldiers charging towards us in a hail of bullets and grenades. The enemy was soon to be assisted by the Luftwaffe, who circled above, before the Stuka bombers descended to strafe. The order to charge was given.

In the chaos that followed, the shouting and screaming became more and more intense. Some men opened fire with an unreal air of calm, while others got caught up in an agitated frenzy, shooting indiscriminately, with little care for themselves.

When blood falls on mud, it changes colour. There is a deep and heavy darkness that envelops it. I was to see bloody entrails spilling forth while their stunned owners paused in disbelief. Eyes were blown from sockets by the blast of explosions. Men on both sides engaged in fierce, close-combat fighting, while all around us was the sound of cranking engines and the noise of mortar shells, machine gunfire, grunts, screams and the last-breath sighs of falling men. The hue of grey smoke did little to mask the horror of the sight of men strewn on the dark-red mud.

At that moment, my only thought was survival. I would do whatever I could to stay alive. I began to move towards a thicket of bushes when a grenade blasted beside me. I felt something pierce my leg with an intense burning sensation. Before I realised what had happened, a German soldier, rifle aimed, was charging towards me. Suddenly, I saw him drop to his knees and fold to the ground. Someone behind me had shot him directly in the chest.

The pain in my leg was unbearable. I writhed in agony and shock.

'Tommy, Tommy! C'mon lad, we've gotta move. We've got to get you back.' As I regained some composure, I opened my eyes to see Ronnie dragging me by the lapels, his bellowing muffled by the buzzing in my ears from the noise of the explosion. He somehow managed to get me back to safety on his own. I was taken by orderlies from the front line, where I was attended to and subsequently moved back to Abbeville.

The following morning, when I awoke, I was still in severe pain. The doctor told me that they had been unable to remove all the shrapnel, but that they had cleaned and closed the wound as best they could. They then explained that after some weeks' rest, I could rejoin my regiment.

I learned that our offensive had been a disaster. We had suffered major losses. Nearly seven hundred men were killed, and many hundreds more were injured. As I lay on my stretcher at the makeshift infirmary, I knew I was one of the lucky ones. The French Army had been no match for the might of the German forces.

That night, I pondered the barbarism of it all. So many men mown down. These were real people who, just like me, only the day before had set out with fear in their bellies and hope in their hearts. Boys and men who yearned for the day it would all be over, and they could reunite with their families and loved ones. Yes, all was now over for them, poor devils. Sadly, they would never again enjoy the warmth of their families' comfort. The flame of life had been cruelly extinguished.

A few weeks later, I was moved back to base where I met with my unit and was glad to see that all my friends had made it.

'Glad to see you, Tommy,' said Frank.

'Me too! We thought we had lost you there for a while,' said Jim.

'Well look who's here, little General Spud himself!' said Ronnie. Our eyes met, but this time it was different. From my bed I stretched out an arm and opened my hand. Ronnie, as if begrudgingly, shuffled forward a few steps. We shook hands. I looked at him and said, 'Thank you.'

Ronnie leaned forward, put his head next to mine and whispered in my ear, 'You and me are very, very different, lad, but when we're out there meetin' those fuckers, well, I suppose we're pretty much the same. We now have to just keep goin' until this shit is over and get out of this inferno as quick as we can.' As he rose, a wry smile crossed his face. I nodded and he walked away.

Although our morale was in tatters, we were buoyed to hear the news that we were to retreat to the coast. The hope of a possible rescue by the navy gave us great encouragement to keep going. At this stage, exhaustion had overtaken us, physically and mentally. Everyone marched with vacant expressions, as if in a trance. On the way, we sporadically saw refugees fleeing the German invaders. We witnessed horrific scenes when the Luftwaffe would attack women and children mercilessly, leaving bodies and prams scattered along the roadside.

Through the grapevine, we learned that Rouen had fallen, which resulted in all our food and fuel supplies being cut off. It was then discovered that Le Havre had also suffered the wrath of the Luftwaffe's Junkers and Stukas. As a result, the order was given to head towards the small fishing port of Saint-Valery-en-Caux to again attempt an evacuation. All non-essential equipment was to be jettisoned as we focused all our attention on getting back to British soil as soon as possible. However, our efforts were frustratingly hindered by the horse-drawn transportation of the French Army, which greatly slowed down the retreat.

On 10 June, we reached Saint-Valery-en-Caux with the intention of holding the town until nightfall, when an evacuation would be attempted. In a twist of fate, a German division being led by Field Marshal Erwin Rommel also reached Saint-Valery-en-Caux on the same day and had taken up position on the clifftops overlooking the town. From this vantage-point, they unleashed a barrage of artillery attacks and demolished most of the town within hours of their arrival.

At this stage, after months of battle, the gut-wrenching nerves from fear of what was yet to come had passed. There was but one goal: survival at whatever cost. An offer of surrender was refused in anticipation of an impending evacuation that night. But just as we crammed onto the beach, word came down that the Royal Navy had been hindered in its rescue attempt by the sudden onset of fog and a persistent pounding of artillery fire from the cliffs above the town. We did not want to believe it, but deep down we all knew that this situation was hopeless. So close, so close. A few more hours with clear skies and we would have had a chance. It was not only fog that had descended. A palpable sense of defeat settled heavily on each man's shoulders.

At 11 a.m. the following morning, the order to surrender was given. A general silence befell the regiment. Some bowed their heads and sobbed, others sat in stunned disbelief, contemplating what might be their destiny. Shortly after, German tanks and lorries surrounded us on the beach where only one night before we had clung to our final, desperate hope for salvation. It was not to be.

The following day, we were marched to a field some miles outside of the town, which had been prepared for our reception. Barbed wire was strung all around the field's perimeter. We were weary and hungry as we hauled ourselves through lines of enemy soldiers searching us for any sharp implements. I was delighted when they did not take my treasured silver cigarette case. Some hours later, a German officer arrived and stepped up to a temporary loudspeaker.

'Silence!' he roared. Despite the fact that there were thousands of soldiers in the encampment, an intense silence immediately engulfed us. 'For you, the war is over. You are now prisoners of the Third Reich. The might of the German Army has now taken possession of a large part of Europe. France will fall in days, and after that it is only a matter of time before the United Kingdom will succumb to our power. Nothing can prevent the glorious onward march of the Fatherland. Nothing can stand in the way of our great

Führer. You will do as you are told. If you do, you will be treated well, and you will have every chance of surviving. If you do not, you will suffer the consequences. You will not try to escape. Any attempt and you will be shot. Tomorrow, you leave for Germany. Heil Hitler!'

That night, as the cold air of the Atlantic descended, I wrapped my greatcoat around me as best I could. Some of the men had kept their blankets, but I had left mine behind in Abbeville, as had many others in the misguided optimism that we would be saved by the navy. When I looked up, I could see the stars twinkling through the black velvet curtain on which they were scattered. How many battles had they witnessed? Had they seen my father stuck in a field as I was now? They had seen bad times, but they had also witnessed many good times, and I told myself that there would be more of the latter. There would be times with Mary, with my father and with my poor mother, who must be petrified not knowing anything about my whereabouts.

There and then, I swore to myself that I would survive. I would see my loved ones again, no matter what it took.

4.

THE LONG MARCH
JUNE 1940

The following morning, we were told to line up in a formation of three abreast to begin marching. This line of soldiers stretched for close to two miles. Word spread among the troops that the rest of the BEF had been evacuated successfully from Dunkirk. The very same coastline and such similar circumstances, yet the delight of one group and the agony of the other could not be further apart. There were thousands of us – haggard, frail, hungry and battle-weary. All our efforts had been for nothing. We knew that we would be taken to Germany but could not imagine our fate.

The Germans were conscious not to take too many of their young, fighting-fit soldiers away from their invading forces. As a result, the number of guards left to watch over us was limited and mainly made up of older soldiers. Though we were treated very harshly, it was nothing compared to the savagery we would soon experience at the hands of the Hitler Youth, who took over some eight days later. We were guarded on each side by armed soldiers, interspersed with others in army vehicles. The march lasted for three weeks, travelling through northern France, Belgium and on to Holland.

Each morning, we were rationed a loaf of bread to be shared among six of us. This, together with a small amount of water, was to last until the next day, but because starvation was so rampant, we always devoured our chunk of bread immediately.

During the march, civilians would try to pass us milk or eggs and, occasionally, soup. Sometimes this generosity was successful but, more often than not, guards knocked the offerings out of our hands. Anyone developing sore feet or blisters had to endure the fierce pain. Any attempt to slow down was met with the butt of a rifle in the face, or worse. Thirst and lice were the two main torments. I prayed for rain in the hope of somehow collecting a few drops to moisten my parched tongue, which was as dry and crinkled as old leather. In the evening, when we stopped for the night, our time was taken up with trying to rid ourselves of the lice that had invaded our bodies. This of course was futile, because by the time we had killed some, it felt as if others had multiplied tenfold.

Attempts to run and escape were dealt with severely. Some men were shot while attempting to do so. Any French soldiers of African descent, especially those from Senegal or Algeria, received particularly brutal treatment.

As soon as we reached a harbour near Rotterdam in Holland we could see a large number of barges lined up and waiting for us. We were given a small amount of bread and told to get on board. We were packed tightly in the cabins, with men on top and men below. I was one of the lucky ones on the top deck. Even though we were all tightly crammed in together, we did not have to endure such stifling heat as those below. There, conditions were so crowded that men had to sleep standing up. The stench of stale urine and excrement made it hard to breathe in the putrid air.

The barges progressed up the Rhine very slowly, the sun scorching during the day. However, by night, the cold on deck was unbearable. Thoughts of food soon returned to torment us. Scraps were sought and sourced from wherever possible. Even mouldy bread was palatable once the lice were scraped off.

After four days, we arrived at the town of Emmerich, in Germany. We were well and truly behind enemy lines. Some hours after our arrival, thousands of us were put on trains to Hemer and, two nights later, my group was put on a train destined for the town of Torun in Poland. Fortunately, most of our regiment was being sent to the same destination. As we sat on the cold, wooden floor of the cattle cart, a whimper was heard from someone at the back: 'I heard that awful things are being done in Poland.' No one said anything. The silence of a cemetery. We all knew what was on each other's mind.

Through the cracks in the wooden slats of the carriage walls, those who still had some strength could see the flow of the vast River Vistula as it meandered its way towards the Baltic Sea. My mind oscillated between the throb of the bleeding blisters on my feet and the gnaw of the hunger cramps in my stomach. Thoughts of Mary only increased my suffering. To make matters worse, every now and then I would feel an excruciating dart of pain from the still-healing shrapnel wound in my leg.

Despite our pitiful state – or perhaps indeed because of it – it was quiet inside the carriage. Only the odd sigh or whine could be heard from the group as the train chugged along, the clickety-clack of its wheels on the tracks distracting us from the anguish of not knowing what lay ahead. We were in a dreadful state. Our limbs felt as though they were merely clinging to our bodies. Toenails had been severed from flesh because of the never-ending pounding of feet. Hair was matted and infested with lice. What was left of our tattered uniforms was smeared with excrement from the constant diarrhoea caused by dysentery. A tin cup was passed from man to man for us to urinate in. When full, it was emptied through a gap in the floorboards. Worst of all, our spirits were broken.

———

It was mid-afternoon when the train came slowly to a stop. The guards jumped out and started to shout orders for us to disembark. As we did, the first sight that caught my eye was the sentry towers. There were four or five of them, all over-looking the bank of the river along which we had pulled to a halt. Each contained several armed guards with machine guns menacingly pointing down towards us. I was overcome with a feeling of vulnerability, not knowing who among us was in their crosshairs at any given moment. Across the river, I could see the outline of the city of Torun, with its red-brick buildings, spires and domes. It was the last time I would see these signs of civilisation for a long, long time.

Once again, we were ordered to line up three in a row. As haggard as we were when we left Saint-Valery-en-Caux, we now looked pitiful. As we began to walk, men hobbled in pain, prodded along by butts of rifles poked into ribs. Thousands of beaten, dishevelled souls marched helplessly along, slaves to their savage, gun-wielding masters.

Over an hour later we reached Stalag XXA, one of several forts constructed around Torun. It was surrounded by a dry moat with armed sentries on either side of the gigantic main gate. As I passed through the gate, I saw there was one large, long main building, which was connected by tunnels to smaller, single-storey buildings. We soon discovered there was a large basement under the main building, which housed 'the cooler' – the cells for solitary confinement. Stalag XXA was enormous, but it remained difficult to spot from the air because the roofs were camouflaged with overgrown vegetation.

The guards divided us into small groups and told us to remove all our clothing. Once we were fully naked, we were herded through a room where we were deloused, before being sent to another room where all our body hair was removed. In fact, this was welcomed by all because it helped to rid us of the endlessly tormenting lice. After a shower, we were handed replacement clothes that were obviously the spoils of war, taken from enemy soldiers and civilians, as reflected in their diverse origins. Later that evening, we were all marched to an area outside Stalag XXA where wooden huts had been erected. We were to be quartered there while the fort was being prepared as our living area.

The next morning, we were taken to a building between the huts and the Stalag. This was the Kommandantur, the Commander's headquarters. It was a formidable building of three levels with thick solid walls. We were told to line up outside and were brought in groups of five into the building to be registered.

Once inside, a guard escorted me into a small, dimly lit room where a German soldier was seated behind a typewriter at a small wooden desk. In broken English, he ordered me to sit down. 'I need to ask you some questions. You will be here for some time, but we hope not too long, because we are winning the war and it may soon be all over. What is your full name?'

'Thomas McGrath.'

'Your date of birth?'

'Seventeenth of January 1904.'

'Serial number?'

'T117287.'

'Rank?'

'Corporal.'

'Religion?'

'Catholic.'

'Address?'

'23 Kingscroft Road, Leatherhead, Surrey.'

'Are your parents alive?'

'Yes.'

'Their address?'

'Coolfin, Portlaw, County Waterford, Ireland.'

He then hung a wooden board with my prisoner-of-war number, 20736, around my neck. I was told to stand with my back to a black wall and my photograph was taken.

———

For a number of weeks, we were confined to the wooden huts. These were basic constructions consisting of four walls and a roof. Each hut was supported by a number of blocks, which left an opening under the floor so that any attempts to escape by digging a tunnel could be easily detected. I gradually became accustomed to the stench from the straw-lined floorboards underfoot. All I could think of was food. My belly ached with the constant pain of starvation. We were given a loaf of bread to be shared among eight men and a small bowl of watery soup as our daily ration, which was even more harsh than what we had endured on the march. Once again, the lice infestation was draining and debilitating. Men cracked lice between their fingernails.

These little creatures helped to bring a form of entertainment and distraction to our lives when a few men organised lice races. They would draw a circle and a selection of lice would be put in the centre. Bets would then be placed on which creature would reach the circle's perimeter first. The 'owner' of the winner would replenish his cigarette ration for a while longer.

At night, as we lay on the hay provided for our beds, covered with blankets or greatcoats that had survived the march, some men could be heard praying to God to help them to survive, while others cursed and swore blindly at the perpetrators of their suffering. Inevitably, talk would turn to food. It seemed as if no other thought would be allowed to enter our collective consciousness. We salivated over mental images of glorious meals we had once enjoyed, or the simple thought of flavours and tastes. Such images were the cause of great torment, but, paradoxically, they provided the blanket of comfort in which the men could wrap their plight and quench it with memories of distant worlds and times gone by.

As I lay there, I prayed to my mother to keep me safe. I thought of my poor Mary. What was she feeling? What was going through her mind? Did she even know that I was alive? The last letter she had received from me was back in March, when I was stationed in Béthune. Then, I had reassured her by saying it would surely be over soon, that we would be reunited. Now, I had no idea if I'd ever see her again.

Oh God, I have to get out of here. Oh dear God, give me the strength to survive this ordeal – help me, please!

5.

PRISONER OF WAR
20736, STALAG XXA
SEPTEMBER 1940

In mid-October, some weeks after registration, we were transferred from the makeshift buildings to Stalag XXA, which I had glimpsed on my arrival. Thankfully, although there were nearly two thousand prisoners, Jim, Frank and I managed to stick together and were allocated the same living quarters. Ronnie was assigned to a room nearby.

Our quarters were small dark rooms, with three-tiered bunks against each wall. In the middle of each room was a table and some shelves, but no chairs. A small embrasure on the front wall allowed a sliver of light to penetrate the room. This was the space in which we thirty men lived and did all that that entails. We cried out, we wept, we ate, we belched and shared the full spectrum of human emotions. At night the rattle of snores, piercing screams and cries of anguish filled the chamber. Men whimpered and sighed, longing for their loved ones back home. At night, exhausted, we would collapse into our thin, hard wooden beds with only a flimsy blanket to cover ourselves. Many were tormented by nightmares and were often violently ill. Others merely grunted and moaned in their sleep. The air was putrid and dank. At night, the only sound that could be heard from outside was that of the bats flapping and clicking. Despite the general squalor, there were very few rats; this was of course because we scavenged everything, leaving no scraps for the rodents.

There was a general air of desolation. We were battle-worn, famished and exhausted. There were sentiments of despair, injustice, and just plain fury that we had not been rescued. There was also a feeling among some that we had been sacrificed and forgotten. This caused bitter exchanges between the men, which of course only added to our pain.

Under the Geneva Convention, POWs with the rank of corporal and above could not be compelled to work. Nevertheless, the Germans did not always adhere to this regulation. While many soldiers were forced into harsh labour or to work under supervision on nearby farms, I decided to volunteer in canteen supplies. My reasoning was that if I refused to work, I might well be transferred to a camp where conditions were far worse. In addition, being close to the food stores and cooking area would probably provide an opportunity for the occasional extra bite to eat.

As the weeks and months went by, a routine of sorts was established. Conditions continued to be harsh and the pain and suffering of the men were severe. The march from Saint-Valery-en-Caux had left many in a state of exhaustion. Our camp conditions did little to improve this and, if anything, only compounded matters. Men developed skin sores and lost teeth. Dysentery, with its gut-gripping cramps, was rampant and turned us into shadows of our former selves. At any given time, hundreds would be lined up to use one of the dozen latrines available for all two thousand of us. Some unfortunates, having relieved themselves, would just walk back down and rejoin the queue.

The little food we were given provided hardly enough nourishment to live on; mouldy bread and potatoes with watery soup made up the daily ration. Men congregated at the bins to scrounge for waste. No vegetable was too rotten to eat, no potato skin too mouldy to chew. Fights and skirmishes were all too common as men clashed over scraps. Some were so weak that they simply gave up and slowly succumbed to their fate. Others existed in a trance-like state, just waiting for the next morsel to come their way.

A further problem that caused huge hardship was that some men did not possess a tin or glass jar in which to collect food, and when bowls were scarce, they had to use their filthy, cupped hands to collect what was available. Theft of food was not uncommon. While it was acceptable and indeed commendable to steal from the enemy, stealing from a comrade would not be tolerated. Incidents of food theft led to the perpetrators' sudden disappearance when caught.

It was so cold that I felt as though the marrow in my bones was turning to ice. The guards told us that the temperature had dropped to below freezing. Stalactites formed on the inside of the chambers, and there was little to warm us as we lay in our bunks at night.

We strove to survive in the face of inadequate food, freezing temperatures, violence and disease. We were lucky in that we did have outdoor yards where we were allowed to wander freely, if only to see the sky, fields and trees around us. Nevertheless, we were under the constant glare of the guards. In the beginning, some of the younger guards were brutal in their treatment. They would scream and beat any man who did not immediately jump to their commands, no matter how feeble the men were. Some guards, however, did show compassion. One of these was Otto.

I was fortunate to have Otto as my immediate overseer in the canteen where I had volunteered to work. The canteen was staffed by five German soldiers whose job it was to make the paltry liquid that was served daily under the guise of soup. They would also disperse bread and potatoes into steel containers, which were then brought to a hall for distribution. That, in effect, was the culinary expertise required of this particular kitchen staff.

It was my job, as part of the supply party, to see to it that supplies did not run low. Whenever we were nearly out of food, Otto would take me and a number of other men to the Kommandantur, outside of the main Stalag, where we would obtain the produce to replenish the stock. On occasion, it was possible for some of us to sneak an extra loaf of bread or some vegetables, however small, under our clothing, to be savoured later. I firmly believe that without this I would have died of starvation.

One day, about six months after our arrival at the Stalag, I was sent to the Kommandantur without explanation. I was ushered into a small room where, behind a desk, sat a young

German officer. In perfect English, he told me to sit down and handed me a cigarette, which I accepted.

'I see that you are Irish,' he said, glancing down at what I presumed were my registration papers. I nodded.

'May I ask – what is an Irishman doing in the British Army fighting a war that is not his?'

'I was living and working in England when I was conscripted.'

He got up from behind his desk and walked slowly around the room. There was silence for a while. He then came and stood in front of me and leaned forward towards my face. Despite his excellent English, he had a strong German accent and his grey-green uniform seemed to somehow amplify his sinister and menacing presence.

'You know, I love history. I have read a lot of history. I know what the English did to the Irish for hundreds of years. They are barbarians and exploiters. Look at what they have done down through the centuries to countless countries that they have plundered to become part of their mighty empire,' he said sarcastically. 'Why should you care? Don't you realise that when we win this war, Ireland will be fully free from the imperial bully? Let me ask you, corporal – if England were again to cause trouble for Ireland, what would you do for the Irish cause?'

I replied in the way I had been told by Sergeant Major Strawbridge, back in Aldershot. 'I am a soldier and, as such, I do not have any choice.'

I learned later that all the Irish soldiers in the camp had been questioned that day. As far as I knew, no one had given in to becoming a collaborator.

Some nights later, we were all awoken by screams coming from one of the adjoining corridors. We could hear the guards shouting loudly in German. It was obvious that someone was being dragged along the corridor. Whoever it was clearly was in a state of terror. Then, suddenly, there was silence.

The following morning we discovered that Ronnie had been captured trying to escape. He was thrown into 'the cooler' in the basement. We were all too aware that some never came out of that cell alive.

Of my friends, Frank, was assigned to a working party that left the camp each day to work on a nearby farm, and Jim Creagan was put in charge of a group working in the graveyard in Torun. Life was harsh, particularly when winter came. None of us had ever experienced anything like the sub-zero temperatures. No matter what you did, you were constantly freezing. This was only made worse by the lack of proper food and the harsh working conditions. Many perished. Some, unable to bear the torment, took their own lives, and Jim had the task of burying them.

Some six weeks after he was caught trying to escape, Ronnie was let out of solitary confinement. Though it was hard to imagine that any of us could lose more weight than we already had, he was now so thin that you could see the bony frame of his ribcage. His eyes bulged from his gaunt face. But solitary confinement had done little to diminish Ronnie's determination to be free. He would wander around telling everyone how he could not bear being locked up and that he had never wanted any part of this war, that he never wanted to be in the army and it had all been a huge mistake. We were concerned for him, and he seemed to worsen with every passing day. He could be seen aimlessly wandering the white-bricked chambers of the fort, his fragile frame clasping the damp walls, his lower lip quivering as he repeated his mantra.

One morning, around a week after he had been released from the cooler, as men were preparing to take up their work duties for the day, we again heard Ronnie ranting at the guards. This went on for about half a minute, the guards screaming at him to stop, when, abruptly, the noise of the shouting was exchanged for that of gunfire. The rapid rat-a-tat-tat of the machine guns stunned us into silence.

As we meekly ambled through the gate to begin our working day, there was a communal intake of breath at the horrific image of Ronnie's bullet-riddled body tangled in the barbed wire fencing that he was trying to climb. Several broken bones jutted awkwardly from his emaciated body. Shreds of tattered, blood-soaked clothing flapped in the wind like gruesome flags. Ronnie's body was still there when we returned to the camp that evening, left hanging for all to see, as a deterrent to others with similar ideas of escaping.

Jim and I often found ourselves engaged in deep conversation, an escape for our minds from the shackles of reality. One night, shortly after Ronnie had been shot, we could not help but try to make sense of the futility of his death.

'Tommy, why do you think he did it? Surely he knew he had no chance.'

'Poor lad, it got to him in the end. It's surprising that it doesn't get us all, you know. He was particularly vulnerable though, as tough as he was. None of us want to be here but we have no choice. It's a matter of survival. Keep your head down and wait for it to pass. The depths that mankind is capable of stooping to never ceases to amaze me. And all for what? So that Herr Hitler can say that his Reich is mightier than the rest? What is it with humans that we can't just coexist in harmony? My father saw it. My eldest brother, Jamesie, saw it. They went through the horrors of the Great War. And look at all the wars going back over the centuries – wars that you and I have never even heard of.'

'You know, Tommy, you have a point there. Westminster dilly-dallied for so long, doing nothing, just allowing the monster to grow. They left things too late and that's why we're here in this shithole not knowing if we'll ever get out and, even if we do, we could return home to find they're all speaking bloody German.'

'Gute Nacht, Jim. Tomorrow is another day.'

———

By the end of 1940 and our first year in the camp, things had become worse. There was an increase in cases of tuberculosis, typhoid and infections from wounds caused by insect bites. It was only in 1941, when Red Cross parcels began to arrive, that our health improved. That same year the camp commander complied with the Geneva Convention and began to permit restricted parcels to be received from family and friends, as well as allowing the highly controlled sending and receiving of postcards on a limited basis. I wrote to Mary and to my parents but didn't know if my cards had been received, since I never got a reply.

Everyone's mental state was fragile. No news from home had led to a general feeling of despair, which was compounded by the lack of information about the progress of the war. All we had were the Jerries' assertions that they were advancing each day towards 'glorious victory', as they put it. What really killed us was not being able to do what civilian prisoners had the luxury of doing, which was marking off the days remaining in prison until freedom. We couldn't do that; we had no idea how long this was going to last. The uncertainty was enough to drive one to despair.

But the Red Cross parcels that arrived once a month were our saviour. Without them, many more men would not have survived. When word spread among the men that parcels had landed, there would be huge excitement around the camp. Their eyes would open wide in anticipation of what was on the way. We reverted to childlike innocence, as if waiting for Santa Claus to come down the chimney, such was the effect of the mental strain that we continued to endure.

Each man received a parcel the size of a shoebox. Though the contents could vary, they usually included leaf tea, condensed milk, sugar, a bar of chocolate, a can of corned beef, sweets, soap and, most treasured of all, cigarettes. Sometimes we'd also get biscuits, which made a splendid treat and were a change from our rotten daily bread.

———

I found out that there had been a number of escape attempts from Stalag XXA in 1940. While a few had been successful, the vast majority had failed. Some men had been shot while on the run, and others, like Airey Neave and Norman Forbes, were captured and sent to Colditz, the notoriously secure camp in Germany. Those very few who had made it went to either Sweden via Danzig or to the Soviet Union, although a warm welcome was never guaranteed in Moscow. The problem was that no one knew what lay beyond the fort and its immediate surroundings. Two other POWs, Anthony Coulthard and Fred Foster, had actually made it all the way to the Swiss border, only to be caught there by a vigilant guard. Some of those who had been recaptured and returned to the Stalag told of wasted efforts to get home while going around in circles for days, not knowing where they were. This was only made more difficult by their lack of Polish or German.

Some mornings, the camp commander, Hauptmann Schubert, would attend the roll call. On occasion he would be accompanied by visiting members of the Gestapo. In fairness to Schubert and the Wehrmacht, they did their best to protect us from falling into the hands of the Gestapo. It was clear to all that the Wehrmacht, the regular German army, were generally not as cruel as Himmler's SS and Gestapo. Had they been so, the consequences inevitably would have been fatal.

Every now and then, Otto, my overseer, and I would sit down between mealtimes. I never knew exactly when I would be called upon to replenish supplies. Otto had very limited English. We had reached an agreement that for every phrase of English I taught him, he would teach me one in German. For months we would sit and slowly help each other to accumulate sufficient vocabulary to at least make ourselves understood in a language that was not native to us. We did become friendly in a way, but I did not trust him.

———

One day, Frank and I were sitting on the grass at the back of the compound. Although the area was busy with lads chatting, there was no one near enough to hear our conversation. The guards were watching us from the roof of the fort but certainly were not within earshot.

'When you are brought out each day to the farms, how far away from the camp do you actually go?' I asked Frank.

He gave me a quizzical look, glanced around to make sure there was no one to overhear him, and said, 'Well, there are three farms where we work. It depends on what needs to be harvested at any particular time of the year.'

'What are the conditions like? Is Jerry on top of you? Do you get to mix with the local Poles?'

'It's usually quite lax. The work is backbreaking, but typically the farmers are grateful and sometimes they let us pick a few vegetables or they give us bread without the guards knowing. They're good people, and I can tell you, they're no friends of the Germans.'

'We saw Torun when we arrived. How far do you think it is from here?'

'I dunno … a mile or two, I guess. Why d'ya ask? Are you planning on seeing the sights?'

'Just wondering, that's all.'

'Well, wonder on, son. I don't think you'll be doing any tourism for a while yet.'

———

As the months passed, we said goodbye to more and more men who, crippled and frail, did not have the strength or will to live. It was such a tragedy and seemed so wasteful. They had endured all that suffering for years, and for what? Jim Creagan was still in charge of the arrangements for burials in the cemetery in Torun. A thankless, harrowing job. There were no grieving relatives, no tears or eloquent eulogies. It was a cold and clinical process that had to be carried out with as little thought as possible. Thinking about it only brought despair.

6.

THE SEED OF A PLAN
JANUARY–FEBRUARY 1942

One of the men in our cell was Hamish Donaldson. He was much older than most of us and exuded an air of understanding that made him stand out. He was from Inverness in the Scottish Highlands. I became very fond of him. There were nights when I would listen to him for hours on end explaining the marvels of the stars and planets. Occasionally, after roll call just before dawn, he would point out to me the constellations that he had described the night before. He told me that he found it quite moving that we had ended up near the city of Torun, the birthplace of Copernicus. On other nights, men would gather round and he would conduct the group in conversation as if he had an orchestra before him. Topics of discussion varied from sport to politics to religion and even philosophy.

On one memorable occasion, someone asked Hamish if he thought that hell could be worse than Stalag. With a furrowed brow, he looked around the group and said, 'Well, I suppose that depends on what your definition of hell might be. For some who are deep believers, they may convince themselves that this here is a mere test, a purgatory to cleanse the soul and prepare for a paradise hereafter.'

'Bollocks!' said Frank. 'I don't believe in any of that crap. It's all gobbledegook made up to control the masses and make people feel safe and cosy with themselves.'

'Well, okay, but let's suppose for a moment that there is a hell,' said Hamish. 'The question is about our concept of hell – do we think that we are worse off here than there?'

'Surely everyone has their own concept of hell,' I interjected. 'To those who believe in religion, it is a place of great suffering and torment, while for others hell can be a state of mind.'

'What do you mean?' Jim asked.

'Well, you know if you've done something wrong, however trivial, it will bother you and niggle you. The greater the wrongdoing, the greater the worry, shame and mental torment that person will endure.'

'But, Tommy, while I understand what you're saying, there are people who commit horrible crimes and it does not worry them one whit,' said Hamish. 'Look at our little friend in Berlin and his cronies; do you think it bothers them in any way, the pain and horrendous suffering they continue to inflict on the world?'

On and on the conversation would flow into the early hours. I was heartbroken when Hamish developed pneumonia and was transferred to a hospital in Torun. We never saw him again. We often wondered if he survived.

———

One morning Otto and I were waiting for orders from the kitchen about supplies to be collected. We were exchanging phrases. At this stage, Otto's English vocabulary had become quite extensive, and he was even capable of limited conversation.

Similarly, I was very pleased with my own progress with German and I felt my confidence grow each day.

'Your country is very beautiful, *ja*? You say very green and lots of seas. Where are the mountains?'

'I'm afraid, Otto, that we really don't have very many high mountains. I think the biggest ones are in the south-west of the country, in Kerry, but I have never been there.'

'Ah, yes, mountains, very good. My country many, many mountains has. You can climb, ah *ja,* very good!'

'Where is that exactly, Otto?'

'Before war, I live in Bavaria. Finish war, I go back fast.'

'Tell me Otto, are there mountains near Torun?'

'Better say Thorn. German name.'

'Yes okay, but what kind of land – you know, ground – is there outside the Stalag?'

'Oh, no mountain. Many trees, what you say?'

'Woods, forest.'

Ja, woods and maybe one or two houses – big wood and big, big river.'

What Otto had no idea of was the seed of a plan that was germinating in my mind. I knew that I had to make an attempt to escape. I really believed that I could do it, provided I made a sufficient effort to think it all through and gather as much information as I could beforehand.

All that we kept hearing from the Jerries was how well the war was going for them. We hadn't any idea whether this was true or not. What we did know was that Hitler and his Nazis were capable of anything and, any day, I felt that an atrocity could befall us all.

I told myself that I should not be afraid to take a chance. If that chance were not taken, I would never know if I could have succeeded or not. That said, fear kept gnawing at me. I knew that once I escaped, a door would be slammed shut. If caught, I would be shot – or worse, my recapture would be hell.

———

As the months rolled by and everyone's health gradually improved, thanks mainly to the Red Cross parcels, we settled into a routine. We also developed ways to entertain ourselves. Some men would read whatever they could get their hands on: a number of books had managed to slip through the censorship of the guards. Other men would play chess with makeshift pieces and boards, while the odd few would break into song, letting their thoughts cling onto the words and sounds so that their imaginations would take them back home to their loved ones.

One night I beckoned Jim Creagan to step outside of our confinement cell to a quiet spot beside the gates of the fort. There was something I wanted to say to him, and I did not want others overhearing me.

'Jim,' I whispered. 'I need your help. Can I ask you some-thing? But you must keep quiet about it, and no one can know.'

'Sure, Tommy, I can keep a secret. What is it?'

'I have a plan. I think I can get out of here.'

'Are you mad? You'll be caught, and God knows what the bastards will do to you!'

'Maybe, but I've got to try. I need your help to get me some civilian clothes. I have already managed to sort shoes, thanks to the Red Cross parcels.'

'Christ, man, are you fucking out of your mind? If you're caught wearing civilian clothes, you'll be shot.'

'I know, but it's a risk I'm willing to take. I've studied the layout and the guards' routine. I think I've a good chance of making it. Will you help me?'

'What exactly do you need, corporal?'

'Thanks, Jim. I knew I could rely on you.'

———

During my daily visits to the Kommandantur, I had noticed that there were very few guards stationed in that area. I had also seen that the edge of the wooded area was flush against a low wall about three hundred yards to the left of the building. I began to think that if I could distract the guards, I could probably make it to the wall, climb over and run into the thick woodland. I would have to deal with what I would find on the other side – but that was for another day.

Some weeks later, Jim let me know that he was working on getting civilian clothes; he had spoken with a trusted Polish woman he met while working in the graveyard, who said she could get me a dark suit. Shortly after that, I took Frank aside and asked him how many contacts he had made in the farms. He said that the families were mostly friendly and repeated what he had told me before: that they hated the Germans.

I asked if there were any children on the farms.

'Why do you ask, lad?'

'They will probably have schoolbooks, but specifically they'll have school maps. I need to get my hands on a map of Torun and its surroundings.'

'What for?'

'I'm looking to the future, Frank, in case we ever need to get out of here in a hurry, you know. We could be bombed – this place doesn't look like a POW camp from above with all the grass they've put on the roof and God knows what the Jerries will do if the Russians or Yanks come knocking at their door. It's good to be armed with a knowledge of the area.'

'You want me to find out?'

'If you can, I'd really appreciate it.'

'Leave it with me, old chap. I'll see what I can do.'

———

Over the next two months, I managed to collect a supply of soap and chocolate from our Red Cross rations. Any cigarettes I received were also secreted away, together with a shaving razor. Towards the end of February 1942, I noticed that supplies were starting to run low in the kitchens. I decided that I needed to finalise the details of my escape in order to be ready for when I would be called on to restock.

Frank had managed to get me a basic school map of the area, which was more than adequate for my requirements. Jim had come up trumps and managed to get a set of civilian clothes from the Polish woman he knew. I exchanged my prized collection of cigarettes for a towel and extra soap, and I raffled my silver cigarette case for 100 Reichsmarks. I hid my supplies behind a loose brick at the back of my bunk. I also quizzed men who had made attempts to escape, and I gleaned a certain amount of information on conditions outside the camp. One man who had been recaptured in Danzig said that it might be possible to get a ship from there. There and then, I decided to head for Danzig.

All I had to do now was wait for the right moment.

7.
THE ESCAPE
MARCH 1942

The ninth of March 1942 was a bright, sunny day. There was a slight breeze rustling through the trees on the fort's perimeter. Although it was still daylight, it would not be long before dusk set in. A handful of us were lying idly about when we got the call to go and draw supplies from the Kommandantur. I had been observing the kitchen supplies gradually dwindling, so I made sure to wear my secretly obtained civilian clothes under my uniform for the last three days, not knowing exactly when we would get the call to restock. I also stuffed the pockets of my inner layer of clothing with all the supplies that I had been storing for my escape.

I stayed at the back of the group of three prisoners as we approached the building. They entered the door ahead of us with two guards, while Otto remained at the entrance. I could see a sentry perched in a watchtower, keeping watch over the Kommandantur and its surroundings. I slowly passed Otto and once inside the hallway, slid quickly in behind the front door without him seeing me.

The hallway was now completely empty. The feeling of the cold stone wall against my back only helped to heighten the tension knotted in my stomach. I could feel my knees tremble and droplets of cold sweat roll down my back. I waited. I knew that it would take at least twenty minutes for the supplies to be sorted. Holding my breath and in silence, I peered through a crack in the door. I prayed that Otto couldn't hear my heart pounding against my chest. Then I saw Otto suddenly leave his position. He walked slowly towards the guardroom adjacent to the building and went in. This was my chance.

With my heart racing, I peered around the side of the door. My luck was in – the guard in the watchtower was distracted and looking in the other direction. I walked first to a latrine area and then, having confirmed that there were no guards about, quickly made my way towards the wall, which I climbed, and then jumped into the the woods. Then I ran and ran like I had never run before. Twigs under my feet snapped while birds scattered and fluttered. A short while later, I heard shouting and a noisy commotion coming from the fort. Eventually, after running with my heart in my mouth for as long as I could, I came across a hole that had probably been dug by Germans and used for training. I jumped in and covered myself with some brushwood, staying as still as possible, my senses taut with fear of hearing the dogs they would send to search for me. I lay there until nightfall.

I had studied the school map provided by Frank and knew more or less what my position was – and so, when I emerged from the hole under the cover of darkness, I headed east first for over half a mile, then north for a while, and then, when I calculated where the direction of the town was, I turned west. Eventually, after coming upon a fence and crossing some barbed wire, I saw a small house in the distance. As I approached in the pitch dark there was no sound other than the pounding in my chest, which to me was deafening. I could barely fend off all the thoughts coursing through my mind. Do I knock on the door? Do I walk on? Or is this whole idea crazy? Should I just turn back and steal into the camp and hope that I hadn't been missed? But I knew I had been. I had heard all the commotion, so I collected myself and took a deep breath.

Ever since I'd been a small boy, I reminded myself, I had never been afraid to take a chance.

I could see no lights at the front of the house, no sign of life, and so I decided to walk around to the back, trying to tiptoe as lightly as possible in order to muffle the sound of the gravel underfoot. Through a small window I could see the flicker of an oil lamp and what looked like the figure of an old man sitting beside a fireplace. I walked back to the front of the house, took a large intake of breath, and knocked twice on the heavy wooden door. I could hardly swallow, I was so nervous. The sound of slowly shuffling feet grew louder until the door opened and I was looking at a heavy-set, elderly man, whose dishevelled grey mane cascaded over his brow. Our eyes locked, mine full of fear, his full of bewilderment. My heart was thumping.

'Do you speak English?'

'*Nein.*'

'*Deutsch?*'

'*Ja.*'

Having spent two years practising with Otto, I now felt

confident to start using what he had taught me. I told the elderly man that I was an Irishman who had been captured while serving in the British Army and that I had escaped from Stalag XXA.

'I am so very sorry to call on you like this. I am desperate, but if you can't help me, I understand and I will be on my way,' I said.

The old man said nothing. His eyelids narrowed and his eyes scanned the wooded area over my shoulder. When he was convinced that I was alone, he opened the door wider and beckoned me in. He pointed to a shaded area, where there was a staircase. He then led the way upstairs.

When we reached the landing, he untangled a rope that was coiled around a grip and pulled open a hatch leading to an attic. He propped a nearby ladder against the wall under the hatch and gestured for me to climb up. With my heart in my mouth, I did as he said. He then closed the hatch and I found myself alone, in total darkness, leaning against the wooden uprights supporting the slanted roof.

My mind was racing. Was I mad? How could I have allowed an old man to trick me into coming into his house and locking me up while he went to raise the alarm? Why would he – or anyone, for that matter – put his own life at risk to help save a stranger? Besides, surely he would get something by way of a reward from the camp guards for behaving as a good Polish citizen.

My gut was telling me not to panic, that all would be well. If I had stayed out in the woods for much longer, it was a certainty that the tracker dogs would have found me. At least here I had a fifty-fifty chance. Besides, there was something in the old man's expression that gave me a comforting assurance that he would help me.

Some time later – it could have been an hour or so – I heard the hatch open. A beam of light shone onto the inside of the roof. I strained my ears to listen for other voices, but there were none. The old man's head appeared through the hatch.

'It is all right,' he said in halting German. 'I do not hear any sounds outside, but you must stay here until it is safe.' He then handed me a loaf of bread with some salami and a cup of warm coffee.

I told him that I had understood what he said, thanked him and put the food and cup of coffee carefully on the floor. As he began his descent, I took hold of his arm with my two hands, looked at his eyes and told him how grateful I was for his help. He stopped for a moment, then nodded, continued down the steps and closed the hatch after him.

———

For the next four days I stayed in the old man's attic. Twice a day he brought me food, and twice a day I would descend the ladder to visit the toilet.

On the morning of the fourth day the old man told me to remove my uniform; he said he was going to burn it. This was a huge step into the unknown for me. I knew that if I were recaptured wearing civilian clothes I would be executed as a spy, but I decided that there was no going back, so I handed over my uniform.

That evening the old man gave me a worn and tattered coat and cap and told me he was going to take me to the nearby town of Torun. Dusk was starting to fall. We walked briskly through the woodland until we reached the Vistula River. From there we followed the gushing water heading north until we reached the lengthy iron railway bridge spanning the river.

The shimmering lights of the town seemed to beckon me as we made our way over the narrow pathway beside the railway tracks. It took nearly twenty minutes to make the crossing. As we approached the end, I froze. There, in front of a sentry box, was a German guard leaning over the rail of the bridge, smoking a cigarette. We could not stop or falter. To do so would surely draw suspicion. Heads lowered, we pushed on. As we neared the guard, to our utter relief, he paid us no attention. Obviously, two country peasants were harmless enough.

We left the bridge and walked on cobblestone laneways through the old part of the town. After about fifteen minutes we came to a busier street that was lined with shops. The

German occupation was in evidence everywhere. Shopfronts were adorned with Nazi regalia. One even had a huge photo of Hitler; the look of insanity in his eyes sent a shiver up my spine.

We approached a door with a sign saying *Okulista*, which I presumed meant an eye specialist. We entered and were guided to a waiting room by a cordial woman wearing a white coat. Shortly afterwards, the oculist, a small, heavy-set man, came into the room and shook our hands.

'I will try help you, but is important that you make as I say. You understand?' he said emphatically in broken English.

'Yes.'

'We not have names. This means safe for you, safe for us.'

'I understand. I am very grateful. Thank you. I really just want to know how to get to Danzig.'

'No, that is not possible. Danzig safe no more. Germans have entered many soldiers. They watch boats, and captains very frightened and give you up. You need be quiet, rest and wait. You understand?'

'Yes, but how long?'

'Maybe weeks, maybe months, I do not know. We go now to different house. Follow please.'

I bade farewell to the old Pole by embracing him and telling him that I would be eternally grateful to him for what he had done for me. He just nodded and said in a low voice in broken German, 'You brave young man, but you go slow, *ja*? You have long time to go. Very strong, yes … then you family, yes.'

With that, we three walked onto the street, and the old Pole turned back towards the bridge. The oculist motioned for me to follow him down a nearby alley.

The aura of the gaslights cast a dim glow on the narrow streets. There were few people around. Some bars were open, and I could see German officers drinking heartily in each other's company. The local populace was nowhere to be seen.

Some twenty minutes later we arrived at Szczytna Street and, halfway down, my companion stopped at a black door. The oculist knocked on the door with what was clearly a signal. The door was opened by a tall, sallow-complexioned man with dark, mournful eyes. He invited us in to a small room, where there were two other men. Both were small in stature, but one was stocky and fair-haired while the other was dark and thin.

The oculist addressed the Polish men, and I could tell that he was recounting my story. They looked me up and down and then moved to a corner to speak among themselves. A little while later they approached me and the tall man asked in perfect English, 'How do we know that you are not a spy?'

'Sir, I can assure you that I am no spy. I was captured at Saint-Valery-en-Caux in June 1940. I was a member of the 51st Highland Regiment that got cut off from the rest of the British Army. I have spent the last two years holed up in that hell across the river known as Stalag XXA. I am Irish and I want to go home to see my wife and my family.'

They exchanged glances with raised eyebrows and pursed lips. There was a silence. No one spoke for what felt like an awfully long time. The taller man then looked at me and, raising his finger ever so slightly, said, 'You know, before the war I lived and worked in England. I was a clerk at the Grand Hotel in Eastbourne. Have you heard of it? It's on the east coast, near Ipswich.'

'Now I'm beginning to wonder who the spy is,' I replied. 'Eastbourne is on the south coast of England and nowhere near Ipswich. I know because our local barman is from there and he never stops talking about the place. Come on, what are you playing at?'

'Very well then – which horse won the Grand National in 1939?'

'It was Workman. I know because I won five pounds on a bet. I backed him because he was ridden by an Irish lad.'

The tall man smiled and put out his hand to shake mine.

'We can help you. The oculist says that you want to go to Danzig. I am afraid that is no longer an option. You must lie low for some time. Tonight we will take you to a safe house. We will contact you once we have prepared false papers. Then we can discuss your best options.'

'Thank you. You are very brave people to risk your lives for me. I can never repay you.'

'We are accustomed to invasions. We have had them for centuries. The Swedes, the Prussians, and even the Russians tried twenty years ago. We are used to it, but each time we will always fight back to regain our homeland until eventually, no matter how long it takes, the invader is quashed and banished from our borders.'

He then gestured to the small, dark-haired man and said that he would accompany me to the safe house. I thanked them all again, and then we left.

The house was located on the outskirts of Torun. Thankfully it was late, and we did not meet any German soldiers. When we'd reached our destination, my companion pointed to a door leading into a block of apartments, which he unlocked. He told me to go up the stairs to the fourth floor, where the owner would be waiting for me. We said our goodbyes and he left.

I climbed the creaky wooden stairs and when I reached the fourth floor gently knocked on the mahogany door. I heard a rustling movement from inside and then light footsteps approaching. The handle turned ever so slowly, and the door eased slightly ajar with just enough space for the owner to ask in a hushed whisper, in Polish, 'Who's there?'

I answered in German that I had been directed to go there and that the owner would be waiting for me. The door opened wider and a voice said softly, 'It's alright, I speak English.'

I stared, speechless.

Before me stood the most beautiful woman I had ever seen.

8.
IN HIDING
MARCH–JUNE 1942

That first night, Lidia had shown me to the smaller bedroom with sparse furniture and a crucifix on the wall. Her flat consisted of a living room, two bedrooms, a kitchen and a bathroom. It was small but not cramped, and it was cold but not freezing. She introduced herself and said that since I would probably be with her for some time, it was impractical for us not to have names. The way she said it led me to believe it was her real name. I felt I could trust Lidia. Each day she would leave the house for several hours and return with whatever food she was able to find.

Throughout those first weeks we hardly spoke. Then, one evening, Lidia asked me to tell her about myself. She invited me to sit down while she made some coffee from ground acorns.

I told her all about where I was from, where I had grown up, my family, and about Mary. I explained how we had moved to England to find employment, and then how I had been conscripted. Her blue eyes seemed to follow my every word. I gave her a brief account of our war experience in France, our capture and the conditions in the Stalag. I did not go into much detail.

Later, when we had finished our coffee, I asked her to tell me about her own life. I could sense the sadness from the way her shoulders subtly stiffened when I asked the question. She slowly raised her faded blue eyes and said, 'It's a complicated story. Maybe at another time.' And with that, we said goodnight.

———

The smell of cordite intertwines with the stench of rotting bodies. Something hard and jagged rests against my brow. I'm puzzled. My mind drifts between clouded images while I grapple to make sense of it all.

I raise my hand. My fingers unclench slowly to reach beside me. Bone. Yes, it's bone for sure. Bone and shreds of matted hair. I freeze. With every sinew in my body I will my eyes to open. There, through a haze before me, is a skull with gaping holes where the eyes had been. And then it explodes with the force of a mortar bomb.

I try to lift my body to move away. I cannot. I am paralysed. I am being pulled down into a swamp of grey and pink dripping intestines. No matter what I do, my limbs refuse to respond. The pain of the wound in my leg is excruciating.

A flood of anxiety engulfs me. My skin is wet from warm sweat, yet I feel icy cold. I am trapped. The horror of it all overcomes me.

I scream.

Somewhere in my subconscious I hear a consoling voice. I feel a gentle hand on my shoulder. 'Tommy, Tommy, it's alright. You're alright. You were having a bad dream. It's over; it's gone.'

I opened my eyes to see Lidia leaning over me, drying the perspiration from my brow with a cloth.

'Thank you,' I managed to say confusedly.

Emerging from the fog in my mind, I continued, 'I am very sorry if I woke you. I don't know why this came over me. Some nights I find it hard to sleep.'

'I know, Tommy. You have been through a lot. It is not easy. I understand.'

She held my hand and knelt beside me. 'Tommy, we must be strong. We must keep going. We have to tell ourselves that this evil that has been visited upon us will not last for ever. You'll see, things will change. We must never give up.'

'Yes Lidia, you are right. We must survive. The world owes you and your comrades in the Resistance so much. You are all so very brave. You are a beacon of hope that will inspire endurance to see us all through this. You give me the confidence to believe that people's humanity and compassion will always overcome savagery and depravation.'

Lidia smiled, stood up and said goodnight with a wistful smile.

———

The weeks passed. When Lidia left the house, she never told me where she was going, and I did not ask. A couple of times per week, she would arrive home with meagre rations of food that she had managed to obtain – she never said from where exactly, though she did say that non-Jewish Poles were allocated a greater ration of food than those Poles who were Jews, albeit still meagre.

Some days I would venture to a nearby alley to do some physical exercise to help recover my fitness after two years in the Stalag. The extent of my exertions was limited because of the throbbing pain in my leg from that godforsaken shrapnel still embedded deep inside, which was often unbearable.

In the evenings I would help Lidia with the housekeeping. I tried not to annoy her by asking too often about when I would receive my new identity papers. She kept me informed of any news she had gathered. She told me that even though the Germans were holding firm on the Western Front, the United States had joined the Allies as a result of the bombing of Pearl Harbor. Some nights Lidia would pour a small tumbler of vodka and we would sit and chat for hours.

One night, after I'd spent about two months in her house, Lidia looked at me and said, 'You only asked me once about my life. For that I thank you. Tommy, you are a good man and I think it is only fair that I tell you a little about myself.

'I was born in a little village not far from Torun. You do know that this is the town's real name, I mean, its Polish name. The Germans changed it to Thorn. My father was a schoolteacher in the local Catholic school and my mother was a seamstress. I did not have any brothers or sisters. We were not rich, but we were not poor either. When I was eighteen, I moved to study in the University of Warsaw. You can imagine the impact that had on a young, innocent country girl. I mean in a good way of course. You must appreciate that very few women were going to university. Shortly before finishing my biochemistry studies, I met Joszef. He was a recently qualified engineer. We fell in love, and six months later we got married. Of course, my parents were not very happy with their only daughter marrying so young and so quickly. However, once they met Joszef, they too fell in love and welcomed him with open arms.

'Joszef obtained a job in Bydgoszcz, a city not too far from Torun. We lived there for three years before the German invasion in 1939. I worked in a small apothecary shop. We were very happy. When the Nazis arrived, the country was in turmoil. Joszef swore that he would do all in his power to help expel them from our country. He joined the Resistance in the hope that it would help stop the Germans.

'At the time there was a sizeable minority of German civilians in Bydgoszcz. Just as news of the invasion reached the town, a number of German saboteurs began firing on the local Polish civilians. Joszef and his comrades retaliated, and quite a few Germans were killed. Unfortunately, he and his group were captured when the Wehrmacht and the Gestapo arrived. They were determined to get revenge. Hundreds and hundreds of innocent civilians and Polish prisoners of war, among them Joszef, were lined up and shot in a mass execution. My father, being a teacher, was sought out and arrested. When my mother protested and tried to prevent his arrest, she was shot and killed. I do not know what happened to my father, and I'm not sure I ever will.'

Once her crying had subsided, I stood up and approached her.

'My dear Lidia, I am so, so sorry. What you have gone through is horrific, and yet you find it in your heart to console me and encourage me ...'

I stepped closer and put my arms around her. I gently embraced her and told her how sorry I was for her, but how very honoured I was to have met a woman of such courage and strength. 'Thank you, Lidia. The world is a better place for you being in it.'

She looked into my eyes and put her arms around me. She pressed tightly against me, and I could feel her firm body as it nestled into my chest. She caressed the back of my neck and moved her lips to mine. My head was spinning, my heart was pounding, my soul was screaming. It had been so long. So, so long. It was as if all that had gone before had suddenly been lifted from my shoulders.

'No, no, Lidia, I can't,' I said as I pulled myself away. 'I'm sorry, but I just can't. I have to return to Mary,' I said, letting my head fall into my cupped hands as I knelt to the ground.

Lidia took me by the hand and said, 'Tommy, it's only you and me. There is no one else here. No one will ever know. I know that you feel for me. I won't tell anyone, and I know that you won't tell anyone either.'

'I won't tell anyone, Lidia, but what will I tell my heart?'

She let go of my hand and said, 'You are a good man, Tommy. A strong and good man. Your wife is very lucky. I hope that you manage to get back safely to her one day. I understand. It's alright. I'm sorry.'

'I'm sorry too, Lidia. Perhaps in another life, at another time. I will never forget you. You have been so very good to me.'

As I lay awake with my head on my pillow, I began to conjure in my mind what had just happened. Her beauty tormented me. Was I a fool to dismiss her advances? Surely there would be no harm in closing our eyes to the horrors of the world. What on earth would become of her?

I also thought about what Poland must have been like when she was a young girl. How her life had changed and been thrown into turmoil.

I tossed and turned in my bed, not knowing how to feel. I thought of Mary and how she must be suffering so much, not knowing where on earth I was. Perhaps by now she might have even reconciled herself to the belief that I had been killed and was at this very moment cradled in her bed, her heart wallowing deep in sorrowful loneliness. Despite all these thoughts, I knew that I would never forget Lidia.

———

During the long hours I spent on my own in the small flat, I often thought of my predicament and wondered if I was crazy to have done what I did by escaping. At least in the Stalag you were unlikely to be shot unless you somehow stepped out of line, even if the conditions were unbearable. However, I knew that now I was a walking target.

I also knew that I was facing an uncertain future, laden with unpredictability. The constant threat of death was omni-present. It was strange to have these feelings while sitting in a small yet comfortable room, the likes of which I had not seen for years.

I wondered how my pals had reacted when they heard the news of my escape. I had told no one but Jim Creagan and knew that he could be trusted not to say anything to anyone. I believed that they would have been happy that I hadn't been recaptured – so far, anyway.

I pondered how Mary was coping back in Leatherhead. How was she holding up? I knew that Dr and Mrs Maxwell were kind people and that they would care for her. My heart sank when I thought of how lonely she must be. It broke my heart that we could not write to each other. In my mind, I must have written dozens of letters, but I knew it would be useless to even try to send any under the German-controlled limited postal services.

At times my mind would drift to Portlaw, a place worlds apart from where I now found myself – a town in eastern Europe mired in disorder and human suffering. Had the war affected my family and friends? Did my father still rise each day at six, as was his custom, to walk through the vast forest on Lord Waterford's estate? And my mother, ever toiling, washing clothes that would never dry in the inclement weather, and preparing meals for the family over the open stove. Her back no doubt stooped that little bit more with the worry of my absence.

Growing up, I always dreamed of the day when I would leave. Go find the real world, I said to myself. Well, boy, more real than this you can never get! How fickle life is. Here I was, hidden away in a stranger's home, in a land I had hardly known existed, having just escaped from the hellhole where I was held captive while fighting for a country that wasn't even my own.

I began to think of the quirks of life. We are born into this world and our destiny lies in the fall of dice as thrown from the hand of God. What if I had been born a German? Would I now be marching for the Fatherland, convinced that I belonged to a superior race?

My frustration was tempered by acknowledging to myself that I was where I was and that there was nothing more I could do other than what I was doing. I told myself that I must focus on one thing and one thing alone, and that was survival.

On her return home one evening, Lidia came into the kitchen, slowly took off her coat and laid it on the back of a chair. She moved towards the sink and placed her outstretched hands on it. I approached her because I had a feeling that something was wrong. When I got near, she turned to look at me and, through eyes that were red from crying, she explained that her contacts in the Resistance had told her that I was to be moved on. This meant we would soon say our final goodbyes. Without a word, we embraced. My heart was torn. One part of me was thrilled with the news that I would shortly be moving on, away from Torun and on to somewhere closer to home. The other part of me was steeped in melancholy, knowing that I would be leaving behind this woman whom I had got to know so well and whom I would probably never meet again.

9.
FARTHER BEHIND ENEMY LINES JUNE 1942

Had it been any other time, I would have perhaps enjoyed the experience of being on a train. Although the seats were threadbare, they were comfortable. The carriage was packed with soldiers returning from the Eastern Front, some of them wounded and all exhausted. There were also some Polish civilians who had been forced to supplement the labour force, on their way to work in Germany, where all able-bodied men had been recruited to fight in the war.

The lighting in the ceiling was dim enough to allow me to gaze out through the smudged windows into the blackness of night and stare up at the stars in their constellations, which were brighter than ever. I took that to be a good sign.

My covert companion, Oskar, and I had been travelling for just over two hours when, out of nowhere, there was a jolt and, with a clanking of metal and swishing of steam, the train screeched ever so slowly to a stop. I heard the handle of the door being opened, and a gush of chilled air rushed through the carriage as the door swung open.

I could see that he was a senior officer by his confident gait. This was further enhanced by the iron cross that he wore around his neck. He was accompanied by two men of smaller stature, both dressed in black, full-length leather overcoats. Gestapo.

They slowly began to make their way through the carriage, stopping to ask random passengers for their papers. As planned, I would pretend that I was asleep in the hope that they would pay us no attention. This was not to be.

The officer stopped at the row in front of us and began to scrutinise the papers of an elderly man. Meanwhile, one of the other two agents approached Oskar and asked to see his papers. He handed them over. The Gestapo agent slowly looked at them and asked in German where we were going, to which my companion replied, 'To Berlin – we have work waiting for us there.'

'What about him?'

'He's with me. We're both going to the same place to work.'

With that, Oskar gently nudged me as if to wake me. I feigned startled surprise and began to sit up straight. My papers were handed over.

'How long are you going to Berlin for?'

'We don't know. A long time, we hope,' I said in German.

In my mind I was anxiously praying that he would not engage me in a lengthy conversation. He nodded and started to hand back our papers, but before we could reach them they were grabbed by the officer who had finished with the old man and was now alongside our row. He studied the papers for what seemed an age, every so often raising his eyes to take a glimpse at the two of us. Eventually, he appeared satisfied and, handing the papers back, he wished us good-night in Polish. *'Dobranoc!'*

I thanked him. *'Dziękuję.'*

My heart was in my mouth as he turned and walked away.

———

Two nights earlier the small, dark-haired man had come to Lidia's home, bringing with him 300 Reichsmarks, a suit of clothes and a working book. This was a brown-covered passbook issued by the German authorities to Poles who had been granted permission to travel outside of their area of residence. It did not contain an identity photograph.

He told me that we would be leaving the following night and taking the midnight train to Berlin. We would be travelling as emigrant Poles, whose lives had been disrupted in Poland since the war, on their way to work in Germany. He was to be Oskar Kowalski and my papers recorded me as Tomasz Mazur. I thanked him profusely and said that I was eternally grateful to him and to all his brave friends in the Resistance.

I could not sleep that night. The anxiety of not knowing what lay ahead was unbearable. My imagination was running ahead of itself and in every direction. Maybe I could slip back into the Stalag. Maybe they would forgive me. Maybe – *For Christ's sake, man, get a hold of yourself. You knew this wouldn't be easy. Remember – focus. You can do this.*

The following evening, as I waited for my travelling companion, Lidia gave me a cloth bag containing bread, a towel and my shaving gear. I took her hand and drew her close to my chest, gazing into those striking blue eyes that failed miserably to hide the enormous pain she had endured.

'There are no words that can say how grateful I am to you. You are a kind and courageous woman. I will be forever indebted to you.'

'We must do what we can in the circumstances that life presents us with. What is the alternative – to give up? I don't think that is an option. My country has suffered for centuries at the hands of invaders. If we did not resist, we would cease to exist as a country and be downtrodden for ever.' She reached her arm around my neck and continued:

'Tommy, you are just like me. You are a survivor. You know how to fight for what is right. You have shown your will to live and escape to return to freedom and your family. You are a good man, and I will miss you so much.'

We hugged for one ever so blissful moment. I held her tight, then drew back and whispered, 'Lidia, thank you for everything.'

There was a knock on the door. It was time for me to leave.

———

In the early morning of Wednesday, 3 June our train eased its way into Berlin Anhalter Bahnhof, the main railway station and terminus.

My palms were sweating. Here I was, deep in enemy territory. I had protested when they told me that we were to go to Berlin. Lidia's contacts had said that it was the safest option because they had a network of experienced agents who were the best people to help me on my way.

As the train came to a stop, Oskar told me that he would soon be leaving me with a man called Pawel, who would take over once we got to the city centre. I admired the calm, efficient manner in which Oskar handled himself throughout this extremely dangerous exercise. He had told me that before the war he had worked in Germany, where the rise of Nazism had provided opportunities for employment. This was where he had obtained a good grasp of the German language. He confided that, in 1939, when Poland was invaded and count-less inhumane atrocities were inflicted on its people, he decided to return home to join the Resistance.

When the train stopped, it was shortly after rush hour and the station was busy. As we spilled out onto the platform, our senses were engulfed in the screeching of steel on steel, the hissing of steam and the smell of oil. We could see armed guards at the top of the platform, checking travellers' papers. My stomach knotted once again. My heart pounded and a magnetic force pulled on every muscle in my limbs to hold them back but, nevertheless, I strode forward and joined the queue that was now forming.

'Papers!'

'Yes, of course,' I said in German.

The young officer looked over the papers and was about to ask me something when someone shouted, '*Heydrich ist tot!*'

Under his breath, Oskar whispered in German, 'They're saying that Heydrich has died!'

The soldiers exchanged puzzled glances. We could see the incredulity in their eyes. Now distracted, unsure of what was going on, our papers were handed back to us without further scrutiny, and we were quickly ushered along.

'What was that all about?' I asked Oskar once we were safely out of earshot.

'I'm not sure, but I know that Reinhard Heydrich is one of the highest-ranking Nazi leaders and he was ambushed a few days ago in Prague. There will be major reprisals now. He is very close to Hitler.'

We got on the underground and reached Friedrichstrasse Station in just under half an hour. We raced up the metal stairway of the station and joined the crowds on the bustling street outside.

I was amazed at how normal everyday life seemed. Yes, there were some buildings that had clearly been damaged in air-raid attacks, but there was no trace of panic in the people. Mothers pushed prams and carried shopping bags, men walked briskly, smart briefcases under their arms, while other workers hauled goods from the backs of delivery lorries.

Ubiquitous in this scene were the German soldiers and offi-cers, but they were not threatening at all – in fact, if anything, it was the opposite. They were on home territory, after all.

We walked towards Unter den Linden, a wide avenue lined with linden trees and elegant buildings, a few of which lay in ruins. The shops had sparse, though colourful, window displays. Every so often we came across cafés with tables outside, which were busy with customers enjoying mid-morning refreshments. At the end of the long avenue, I could see an impressive archway crowned with several enor-mous statues.

'That's the Brandenburg Gate,' Oskar said. 'At the other side of it there is what's left of the Reichstag, the parliament building that was burned down shortly after Hitler came to power. They say he organised the fire himself so that he could blame the communists, have them eliminated, and enable the Nazi party to seize total power and at the same time suppress democracy.'

We turned off Unter den Linden and into a small side street, where Oskar gestured towards a café and an outside table.

'Come, sit down here. We will wait for Pawel.' The waiter came up and Oskar asked him for two coffees. When they arrived, I took a careful sip. The rich, bittersweet flavour was staggering. I had never tasted anything like it. I put down my cup and held my head in my hands.

'What's wrong, comrade? Is the coffee not good for you?' asked Oskar.

'Do you know what my friends are drinking and eating in Stalag as we speak?' I sighed.

His eyes were compassionate as he nodded. 'I know.'

Suddenly, it was as if something within me had deflated. My temples began to throb, the back of my neck retracted like a coiled wire, and I felt an enormous strain pressing down on my shoulders. It was as if I were being crushed alive.

'Do you know, Oskar, if they're lucky, they just might find a piece of raw, black potato in the filthy water they call soup? The loaf of bread that is thrown to us to share is also black and rotten. The hunger pains in our stomachs constantly gnaw away at our souls. The only distraction from that particular and persistent torment is the lice that infest our bodies as we wade in pools of human waste.'

I was about to continue when I heard someone say hello.

'This is Pawel,' said Oskar as a tall, well-built young man sat down beside us. We shook hands.

Pawel warned us that we would have to exercise extreme caution because there was an increased level of military activity around the city. A funeral ceremony was to take place later in the week for Reinhard Heydrich.

'You must leave with Pawel now,' Oskar said.

I placed my hand on his arm and said, 'Oskar, I am sorry – it has been very tough for me. I've gone through years of constant torturous exhaustion. I am living from day to day not knowing what lurks behind every corner. But when I remember the lads I left behind, it pains me deeply. I get overcome by anger and it just gets to me.'

'I understand, but it's behind you now. You must keep strong!'

'I will, thank you.' I felt utterly despondent and alone at that minute.

'You know, we put our lives at risk for people like you so that one day we may be free again. We don't need to hear your stories of what you've been through, or that you're feeling sorry for yourselves. My people are no strangers to the brutalities of the Third Reich either!'

'I am very grateful, Oskar. Thank you,' I said as we shook hands.

Pawel and I walked back to the underground station and took a train to another part of the city. We were asked for our papers before boarding the train and got by without trouble. The journey took around fifteen minutes. From there we walked to Pawel's home, crossing several cobbled streets. We encountered few people, with only the occasional car or bicycle passing us by.

From outside, the grey apartment block looked run-down. The wooden steps leading to apartment 4B creaked from age. Pawel unlocked the shabby wooden door and gestured for me to enter ahead of him. As I did, a small boy ran from the hall into the kitchen to hide behind his mother, who was clearly busy preparing food over a stove.

'This is my wife, Katarzyna,' said Pawel. 'And this little fellow is our son, Emil.'

'Hello, pleased to meet you. Forgive me for intruding into your home like this. I am so very grateful to you. You are all so brave. Without you I would never have a chance to survive.'

'We will do what we can to help you, but you must be very careful. Remember, it is not only your safety that is at risk now,' Katarzyna said, placing her hand on Emil's small shoulder.

'Don't worry, I will.'

10.

THE LION'S DEN
JUNE–AUGUST 1942

O ver the course of the next few days, I settled in with my new hosts. I helped with some of the household chores and did whatever I could to assist. Even though I had to keep a low profile, there were times when I needed to venture out into the neighbourhood to get some fresh air and stretch my legs. It was a poor area and some of the buildings, which were already in a decrepit state, had been further damaged by the night-time RAF aerial attacks. In the evenings we would sit around the table to share whatever meal Katarzyna had prepared. The couple told me that they had come to Berlin from Poland some years before the war broke out and that Pawel had secured a good job in an automobile factory that had now been taken over for the production of armoured machines for the war. Shortly after this, Pawel felt that he was under suspicion owing to the heightened security, so he had moved to his present address out in the suburbs where his presence was less conspicuous among the locals.

A few days after my arrival, Pawel asked me to accompany him to the other side of the city. He wanted me to meet another member of the Resistance who just might be able to get me out of Berlin sooner than they had thought possible.

We took a tram into the city centre and from there we intended to take another to our destination. However, as we were about to board the next tram, we were engulfed by a swarm of people all heading in the same direction.

We decided to join the crowd so as not to draw attention to ourselves. It did not take us long to realise that we were witnessing the commencement of the funeral ceremony of Reinhard Heydrich. The whole area was thronged with members of the German military, many of whom were in full decorative uniform. Pawel and I stood and watched as the funeral cortège passed by. I was stunned to see ordinary people raise their arms to give the Nazi salute, while more than one visibly wiped away tears. It was clear that this regime, which had set its sights on conquering Europe, had the total support of the German people.

We were to meet with Pawel's contact in a bar some fifteen minutes' walk from the city centre. On the way, soldiers stopped us and asked for our papers. I sighed with relief once we had been waved on. Being constantly stopped paralysed me inside. It felt inevitable that at some stage I would be found out.

While planning my escape in the Stalag, I had dreaded the thought of being stopped at checkpoints. However, the fear I felt back then was nothing compared to the reality of cold sweat forming on my brow, my heart pounding through my ribcage, and my legs weakening, all while trying not to flinch under the glare of a scrutinising guard. At each and every checkpoint I was sure that this time my luck would run out.

As we reached the top of the narrow street where we were to meet, we could see a commotion at the door of the bar. Soldiers were standing at the entrance while others were rushing in and out. We retreated into a doorway so as not to be seen.

An army van approached from the other end of the street and pulled up at the entrance of the bar. A short while later a number of heavily armed soldiers emerged with two men in shackles. Pawel cursed and whispered to me that one of them was the man we were to meet. He was very active in the Resistance and had been on a wanted list for some time.

Although the soldiers were down a small hill at a distance, we both knew that we had to disappear immediately. Just then we heard a loud shout: '*HALT!*'

I turned and saw a German officer pointing at us from up the street.

Pawel shouted, 'Run!'

We took off, frantically trying to outrun the soldiers we could hear gaining ground behind us. Shots rang out. Bullets whistled close by. Instinctively, we weaved from side to side in an effort to avoid being hit.

After what seemed like a long time darting down laneways and back alleys, but which must only have been minutes, we reached the River Spree, having managed to put some distance between us and our pursuers. I followed Pawel down stone steps leading under a bridge. Breathing heavily, he said, 'We have to split up. You go on, I'll go this way.' He pointed in one direction and took off in another.

I didn't have time to argue. Panicked and despairing, I ran along the side of the wall hugging the quay, then ducked into an alcove under an arch. I listened. I could hear nothing to indicate that the soldiers had followed us.

Looking around for somewhere to hide, I decided there and then that my best bet was to bide my time and wait for the cover of nightfall before re-emerging. I managed to crouch in a dark corner of the alcove. The minutes passed and my rasping breaths subsided. The sweat on my brow cooled and dried. More time elapsed. I waited and waited. What was I doing here? What kind of a fool would do such a thing? I was in the heart of Berlin – the lion's den.

After several hours, once it was fully dark, I decided to make a move. I had to get back to the safety of Pawel's home. But how? I had a vague idea of an address, but I could not remember the name of the train stop to get to it.

I slowly eased myself down from my perch under the quay and peeked out of the alcove. The silvery water flowed slowly under the bridge. Tongues of spray licked the sides of the small boats that lay anchored beside the moss-covered, concrete walls. I decided to continue along the water's edge for as long as I could. At least down at river level there was less activity and less chance for me to be seen.

After ten minutes or so, I reached another bridge and decided to climb the iron ladder on the wall to get some idea of what lay above. It was late. There was little traffic and very few people around. I could see glimmering light coming from two or three bars, all of which were half-empty. It looked safe for me to proceed.

I had no idea where on earth I was. I decided that the only thing I could do was to get back to the train station at Friedrichstrasse. At least from there I was sure that I would recognise the route that Pawel and I had taken days before.

I started to walk in what I hoped was the right direction. Some minutes later, I saw a couple strolling along a street lined with shops which, because it was late at night, were closed and had their windows blacked out in case of air raids. I followed them for a minute or so and when they stopped to cross a road, I approached.

'*Guten Abend*,' I said cheerfully. In the best German accent I could muster, I continued, 'Can you help me, please? I need to get to Friedrichstrasse and I'm not really sure of the way.'

They turned to face me. I could see that under the man's raincoat he was wearing the uniform of a German officer. He scowled.

'Who are you? What are you doing out here alone?'

'Well, you see myself and my friends had come to pay our respects to Herr Heydrich but with so many people ...'

His eyes narrowed. 'Papers!' he hissed.

'Oh Klaus, can you just leave the poor man alone? Don't you see he's lost? Come on, we're out for an evening stroll. Leave him be.'

Reluctantly the officer turned, took the arm of his companion and walked away.

I ambled through the dimly lit streets for what felt like hours. I became more cautious. Any time I saw someone, I turned onto a side street. Meeting that officer had made me realise how vulnerable I was.

As the tinge of dawn announced that the next day had arrived, I came upon a horse and cart being driven by an old man. He wore a light linen coat and a cap, which was pulled slightly to one side of his grey hair and craggy face. An unlit cigarette dangled from his lips. 'Friedrichstrasse?' I asked.

He looked down at me and said nothing.

'Friedrichstrasse?' I repeated.

He removed a worn blanket that was lying next to him on the wooden seat and tossed it on top of some bags of coal in his cart. I climbed up and sat beside him.

The clip-clop of the horse's iron-clad hooves was magnified by the hard surface of the cobblestoned road. The dimly lit streets were bare, but for a few passers-by and one drunken wanderer, clearly oblivious of the harsh realities of the world going on around him. As we trundled slowly along, through the branches of the passing trees, I could see a dimly lit bar with workmen preparing for the harsh day ahead with ersatz coffee and schnapps. Occasionally, the ubiquitous German soldiers could be seen in small groups keeping vigil at some street corners. The coal man's face showed no emotion throughout. With his head half bowed, the same smokeless cigarette still dangling. He said not a word. Twenty minutes or so later, I began to recognise the area, so I descended from the cart and thanked the driver, who just looked at me and moved on.

I recognised the avenue where Oskar had pointed out the impressive archway some days earlier. From there I could find the train station. I boarded a train heading north and sat beside the window to search for anything that would jog my memory about where I had got off the train with Pawel. A few stops farther on, I recognised the name of the station, Hennigsdorf, emblazoned on white metal signage with black Gothic lettering.

I got off the train and managed to retrace my steps. Soon I was climbing up that same wooden staircase to knock on the door of 4B. Katarzyna answered.

'Oh Tommy, thank God you've got here. Are you alright? We were so worried. Pawel got home and told me what happened. He said you had to split up and he felt so ashamed that he had left you.'

'It was an interesting evening in Berlin, but one that I'd rather not repeat,' I said with a wry smile. 'And please, Katarzyna – he did the right thing. It was the only way we could make it out of that situation alive.'

Katarzyna brought me into the small kitchen. Emil clutched her skirt, following closely. She told me that Pawel would be home in a few hours and that I should rest, but first she insisted that I eat some boiled eggs and bread. She said that she had been to the grocer's the day before and had used her ration stamps to replenish the sparse kitchen cupboards. Feeling guilty, I agreed that I would accept one egg and a piece of bread, because I was famished. Although a familiar feeling, these hunger spasms were still a far cry from what I had endured at the Stalag.

Later that night, I awoke from a deep sleep to find Pawel standing at the small bedroom door. He gestured for me to join him in the kitchen. He poured a bottle of beer into two glasses, handed me one and winked. 'As you say, cheers!'

'Cheers! And as we say in my old country, *sláinte*!'

He handed me a cigarette, which I lit with a match from the box on the kitchen sideboard.

'They arrested Stefan, the man we were going to meet yesterday,' Pawel said. 'As you know, they're clamping down on the Resistance and he was a wanted man. He has been a thorn in the sides of the Nazis for years. He successfully carried out sabotage attacks on arms-storage depots and railway lines and has been head of the Resistance in Berlin for the last year. He will be sorely missed. Although Heydrich's assassination has had nothing to do with us, there has been increased military activity, by the Gestapo in particular. We heard that in Bohemia they have murdered hundreds of men, women and children and burned down villages as a reprisal.

These men are worse than animals! They will brutally torture Stefan before they kill him. But he is strong. He will tell them nothing. But there are others who may have been caught who will not endure what they will be subjected to.'

'Does Stefan know where you live?' I asked.

'No, we share as little personal information as possible, precisely for that reason.'

'What can I do to help?'

'Nothing, but you must not leave the house again, or if you have to, you must not go alone.'

'I understand. I'm sorry about your friend Stefan, and I'm sorry that I am imposing on you. If you wish, I will leave and …'

'And do what? Where would you go? They would have you within an hour. And then what? They will shoot you or send you to a concentration camp. No, no, Tommy, you stay here. We'll get you out when the time is right.'

'All I can say is thank you, to both you and Katarzyna.'

The days passed slowly; the hours seemed to pass even slower. Each day I continued to help Katarzyna with various chores around the apartment or assisted Pawel with some repairs.

I also helped mind little Emil and we soon adopted a ritual where I would tell him stories to help him go to sleep. I had to use a lot of hand signals and theatrics to relate what I was saying, but he seemed to understand me. I described playing hurling for the local team back home, our adventures in the woods, the ghost stories that my father told us around the kitchen fire, but these had to stop when Katarzyna heard about them and gave me a scolding for scaring the little fellow. She did half-smile when doing so, though. I think she preferred the story of the little boy in the tiny boat lost at sea in the dark during a storm. Especially the part when his dad arrives to save the day!

Every so often, the air-raid sirens around the city would alert people to an impending air attack. The resulting destruction from the aerial bombardment was clear to see in the adjoining neighbourhoods, particularly wherever there was industry. Fortunately, there was very little damage done to the immediate area where I was in hiding.

At the beginning of August, Pawel arrived home with an *Ausweis*, an identity card issued by the Germans. It was made out in the name of a Frenchman named Frédéric Martin. Unlike the more basic identity papers I was given in Poland, this document contained a photograph of someone who bore a slight resemblance to me. The card was the type issued to foreign workers in Germany. My host also gave me a yellow leaflet bearing the word *Sonderzug*. This was a pass for use only on special trains. Underneath were three stamps and the name of the German firm Siemens. Pawel told me that the documents had been issued to a French worker going home to Dijon on leave.

'I presume there is no possibility of Monsieur Martin showing up on this train at the same time as me?' I asked, half-joking.

He smiled. 'That will not happen. How we got these is of no concern to you, but Monsieur Martin is French, and I assure you that he is safe – no holiday, yes, but safe!'

That night, Katarzyna got to work on my hair. She washed it and spent an hour styling it until it looked exactly like the photo on the ID card.

'Voilà! Monsieur Martin!' she grinned as we admired her handiwork in the mirror.

I gave Pawel all the money I had, which was about 400 Reichsmarks. The following morning he went to the train station and bought me a ticket to Paris. That evening I bade farewell to Emil and thanked Katarzyna for her kindness. I wished her well, and Pawel and I left.

He took me to Potsdamer Bahnhof, where there was a crowd of about seven or eight hundred Frenchmen huddled, waiting to board. After a few minutes, I was introduced to a Parisian with whom I was to travel. I gave Pawel a firm embrace and thanked him once again before he turned and vanished into the crowd like a drop in the ocean.

The Frenchman and I mingled among the group. I kept my head low, not wanting to make eye contact with anyone. We boarded the train at 6.30 and at 6.45 the sound of the stationmaster's whistle blew, and the train rolled gently forward as we began our journey to Paris.

11.

MONSIEUR MARTIN
AUGUST–DECEMBER 1942

Just after dawn we stopped in the town of Hamm, and I bought a coffee. I had managed to sleep, on and off, throughout the night. My French companion, who spoke no German and had only some words of English, occasionally exchanged a few words with some of his fellow countrymen. At around noon we arrived at Herzogenrath on the Dutch border. Owing to the damage that had been inflicted by RAF air raids, we all had to leave the train while it was shunted to another platform; in order to rejoin it, we had to pass through a subway, where our tickets and identity cards were again checked. Luckily, mine were approved with a cursory glance from the guard. We then continued our journey to Paris via Maastricht and Namur. We reached Paris at 9 p.m. on 8 August.

As the train pulled into Gare de l'Est in Paris, I felt a huge sense of relief to have left behind the stifling pressure of living so close to the enemy. Even though there was still evidence of a strong German presence in Paris – Nazi flags and banners drooped ominously throughout the station – I immediately felt better and began to enjoy the different atmosphere and fragrances in the air. My companion struggled to communicate a message to me in broken English, but I was confident that I understood what he wanted me to do. When we got off the train, we were to go our separate ways. I was to leave the station and look for a café to the left of the building. I would wait there until a lady with a light-blue beret came in and sat down. I was to make myself known by my name, Frédéric Martin. I bade my companion farewell and did as he had instructed.

I mixed with the crowd of travellers, making my way towards the front gates. There were not many German soldiers about and those I did see seemed relaxed. They were obviously enjoying their easy station in France and were under little pressure since the war was going so well for them.

I walked through the front gates and into the crisp evening air. People scurried around as if they were all in a rush to be somewhere. I caught a glimpse of a dimly lit café on a corner to my left and walked towards it.

I could see through the beige lace curtains of the windows that there were only a handful of patrons sitting at the few tiny tables in front of the bar counter. I decided to venture in.

'*Pardon monsieur, fermé, fermé!*' said an elderly waiter dressed in a white apron with a cloth over his shoulder. I nodded at him and looked around the room.

There! Yes, it had to be. A young woman was seated on her own at a table. On the table rested a dark blue fedora.

But didn't he say a beret? And wasn't it light blue?

No, it had to be her. I must have misunderstood. After all, his English was very poor.

The woman met my eye, raised her head and gave me a faint smile. The waiter, having seen me reciprocate, stepped back and let me go by.

'Frédéric Martin!' I said as I extended my hand.

To my surprise, the woman stood up abruptly and gestured towards the door.

I followed her in silence to a nearby side street until we reached the entrance to a shabby, run-down hotel. There, she signalled for me to follow her up the stairs and into a dank, mouldy room. The weak light from the window reflected the grimy wallpaper.

'*Trois cent francs,*' she said, rubbing her thumb over her forefinger.

I was stunned. The realisation of what had happened riveted me to the floor.

'No, no, *pardon*, *le* mistake, *pardon.*'

'*Anglais?* English?'

'Yes, no. I mean no, not English. Irish.'

With that she began to laugh. She raised her hands to her cheeks.

'What are you doing here?' she asked in English, engulfed in her mirth.

'I was to meet a lady in that bar. She was going to help me. I thought that you were her. I'm very sorry. I must leave, I have to go.'

'But you cannot go out! You will be arrested. The *Boche* [†] has imposed a curfew from ten until five in the morning each night. And that's what would happen to a Frenchman. You don't look like a Parisian, nor do I think that you are in

† *Boche* was the slang term used by the French to describe German soldiers.

Paris to see the sights, and I suspect you would be of great interest to our friends, especially the Gestapo.'

I knew that she was right, but what should I do? Tell her everything and risk her betraying me for some small reward, or trust her to help me? In any case, where was I going to go, not having an idea of where I was? Something about this woman intrigued me.

I walked over to the window and moved the faded curtain sufficiently to reveal the narrow street below. It was isolated and gloomy. The glimmer from the solitary streetlight cast an eerie spell over the scene.

I turned my head to look at the woman who was now sitting on the side of the bed.

'How come you speak such good English?' I asked.

'My father ran a successful exporting business in northern France and my parents sent me each summer to stay with friends of theirs in the south of England. That is, until the Great Depression of the 1930s came along and his business collapsed. The banks took everything – our house, car and even my mother's jewellery and fur coat. It was all too much for my father. He took his own life, and my mother died a broken woman ten months later. I was left with nothing. I came to Paris in the hope of finding something, but then war broke out and there were no jobs available. I had to do something to survive, so I did the only thing that I could, and that's why you see me here in this filthy dump.'

'I'm very sorry to hear that. How cruel! Was there no one you could turn to, no one to help?'

'No, no one at all. I am alone in this world, and I must do as I can to live, and when this horrible war is over, no matter how it ends – and it will end someday – then I will take my life back and put all of this down to a bad dream.

'Now – stay. Don't worry, I won't bite! Anyway, I've paid for this room for the night. It's up to you. But if you're going, then go now. I'm tired.'

———

I nodded in and out of slumber, the drip-drip-drip of the water from the tap in the corner marking time. I had ended up sleeping on the chair, which I had placed against the wall beside the window – that way I could rest my feet on the ledge and stretch out. I would pull the thin, worn blanket up over my shoulders, leaving my legs bare and cold. Every now and then I was jolted awake by noises coming from the adjoining rooms.

As morning approached, a sliver of light appeared through the shabby curtain, illuminating the dust motes drifting through the air. Across the room I could make out the contours of the young woman's slender frame under the sheets. *Poor girl!* I thought. *What a waste. But then I suppose she's one of the lucky ones.*

An hour or so later, she woke up. We agreed that I would step out to the bathroom in the hall to wash and shave while she got dressed. The white tiles on the wall enhanced the coldness of the small room. For a while, I stared at a sink-like basin, almost at ground level beside the toilet. Eventually, I realised what it was for. *My God, these French are hygiene fanatics. Imagine, a wash basin just for your feet!* When I got back to the room, the girl was gone. I decided that I could not stay too long in the hotel, so I left. As my papers specifically said that I was on leave to go home to Dijon, I thought that the safest place for me to be was the nearby Gare de Lyon, from where trains departed for Dijon.

Since it was well signposted, I managed to get there in fifteen minutes. In the station, I sat on a bench at the side of a platform that was teeming with travellers going to their various destinations. I tried to make myself as unobtrusive as possible. The hours passed and my mind wrangled with the decision about what to do. I did not have papers to stay in Paris. I knew absolutely no one and had no idea where I was. My head was in my hands, my mind lost in confusion. The next thing I knew was that I was looking at a pair of shiny jackboots. I looked up to see a stocky man in a German military uniform glaring at me.

'*Papiers!*' he demanded in French.

I stood up and retrieved the documents from my pocket. He began to splutter words at me in French and it was clear that he didn't speak it well. I handed my papers over, and he studied them for an uncomfortably long time. I could sense the beads of cold sweat beginning to form on my brow. He raised his eyes and stared directly into mine. He again muttered something in broken French, which I just couldn't understand, even if I had known the language. A moment's silence hung in the air.

What to do? Will I run? I asked myself. No, that would be mad. There are other Germans around who would get me, even if this one missed with the shot he would surely fire.

In German I said, 'My name is Martin. I am on my way to Dijon, on leave from Germany. I work in the Siemens factory in Berlin. It is a beautiful city, and I am treated very well there by the people.'

His expression softened. There was even a hint of a smile. 'That is good to hear. My uncle used to work there. A good company.' To my relief, he handed back the papers, turned around and walked away.

My body collapsed back onto the bench, and I did not move for quite some time.

Once I had recovered from the encounter, I needed to go to the bathroom. I got up and proceeded towards the public toilets. As I passed the station ticket office, something caught my eye. On top of a small suitcase there was a light-blue beret. The suitcase was at the feet of a woman standing at the ticket counter, engaged in conversation with the attendant. I waited until she had finished.

As she turned around, I approached her and said, 'Excuse me, I am Frédéric Martin.'

———

The sun's summer rays danced on the silver ripples of the Seine as we walked along its banks towards Sully-Morland. She had told me to call her Hélène. She had arrived at the café very late the night before. The maître d' had told her I had been there and had left with a woman. She'd suspected what had happened and decided that she would go to Gare de Lyon to see if she could find me, because my papers would not allow me to stray too far from there. When I had spotted her, she had been buying a train ticket to travel to Lyon that evening.

As we walked through the bustling streets, it struck me how resigned the people seemed to be. The capital had been surrendered to the invading forces and yet I could not sense any resentment towards the enemy. Maybe they were just relieved that their city had not been razed to the ground.

Hélène told me that she had grown up in London, where her French parents had moved to when she was a little girl. When war broke out, she was recruited by the Special Operations Executive, thanks to her fluency in French. She was in an ideal position to give support to the local Resistance in Paris.

'Have you heard of the SOE?' she asked.

I shrugged.

'The SOE is a secret organisation of agents set up by the British. Many of us are women because they think we blend in better than men do owing to there being so few men left in the city. If we're caught, it's game over. They torture us before executing us. So you'll understand why I am so cautious.'

I was taken aback, and I gave her a look of admiration. 'So it's not just those who escape who have to watch their backs. We're in this together.'

Halfway down a narrow, run-down street in Sully-Morland, we reached a large wooden door that led into a small fore-court. I followed Hélène up a narrow staircase. On the first floor she knocked three times on a shabby door. A middle-aged man opened it and stepped back to let us in.

'Frédéric, this is Krzysztof Kubica,' Hélène said. We shook hands and he asked us to take a seat.

Hélène explained that Krzysztof had been living in Paris since he had fought with the International Brigade on the republican side in the Spanish Civil War. After the nationalists' victory, he returned to Paris to take up his old job as a waiter.

In measured and clear English, Krzysztof explained that he had been fortunate to get out of Spain, having done what he felt he had a responsibility to do: to try to stop fascism. 'And now, here we go again! I try and do my part to help wherever and whenever I can to assist those facing the scourge of Nazism.'

'Well, I can tell you that I am deeply grateful to you for your help,' I said.

Hélène said that I should stay with Krzysztof until a plan was devised and papers prepared to get me out of France. She said that the Resistance had contacts in Marseilles, who would more than likely put me on a boat from there to North Africa, which, at that time, was a route of choice for many escapers. However, Hélène suspected their contacts had become compromised, so we might have to resort to other avenues.

'Now I must go – I have a train to catch. I strongly urge you not to leave this building for any reason. Krzysztof will bring you food, and when your papers are ready, we will let you know.'

'I really don't know how to thank you. You are saving my life. There are no words that I can say to thank you enough.'

Hélène turned towards the door and opened it. Before leaving, she stopped and turned around, looked at me and said with a serious face, 'You really shouldn't speak to strange women, you know.' She smiled mischievously.

I laughed.

After she had gone, I found myself pondering on how lucky I had been to have been helped by the Resistance. These ordinary men and women, from all walks of life, who day in, day out risked their lives and the lives of their families in order to help others and to seek salvation for their homeland. *No!* I reminded myself. These were not ordinary men and women. They were heroes. They did not opt for the easy way out by turning a blind eye or hiding their heads in the sand. No, sir! These were the people who dignified the essence of humanity.

———

The weeks trundled on. Each morning Krzysztof would leave for an hour and come back with some food. Food rationing had been introduced since the fall of Paris. The bulk of local produce was shipped to Germany and what remained was strictly rationed. Coupons had to be presented when buying certain foods. Fortunately, Krzysztof had a good relationship with the shop owner, who supplied the swanky restaurant where he worked as a waiter. As a result, we were never too short of essentials.

When he left for work, I would spend my time doing exercises to try and continue my physical recovery. The main problem was maintaining my mental stability. The solitude was overwhelming. My only escape was the view of the city's rooftops through the apartment's small windows. From there, I could let my imagination take flight. I could fly like the birds I saw soaring, twirling and diving, just like back home in the forest. I could look out over the rooftops and see the smoke curling and winding its way to the sky. It made me think of the hours spent sitting around the fire on cold winter nights, listening to my grandfather telling stories of days gone by. My only motivation was knowing that one day I would see Mary and my family again. I knew I had to get my old life back and not have the constant threat hanging over me of being shot or, worse, being tortured.

On at least two occasions during my stay, several people called to the apartment to meet with Krzysztof. I was introduced to them. They were members of a cell of Resistance fighters; their leader's *nom de guerre* was Morland, a man in his thirties, with dark, intense eyes and an aquiline nose. Also present was a woman with a prominent limp. She was American and a member of the SOE.

I quickly learned that I should go to my room during their visits. Whatever they had to discuss was not for my ears. Subsequently, my host did describe to me some of the actions that these brave souls carried out to help foil the invaders' reign of terror. These included the gathering of military intelligence to pass on to the Allies, acts of sabotage on transport facilities, and the interruption or even destruction of electrical and telephone networks. The fact that these brave men and women persevered, despite most of their countrymen's resignation to living under Nazi rule, was not only remarkable, it was heroic.

Some nights, when he returned late after work, Krzysztof and I would go down to Café Rivoli on the street corner. There we would sit and talk over a glass of cognac into the early hours of the morning until the owner, Pascal, or his wife, Odette, sent us home. I never knew if Odette was a member of the Resistance or not, but she always seemed particularly friendly towards me – as if she knew.

I told Krzysztof about my background in Ireland and how I had ended up in the British Army. He was horrified at how we had been treated by the Germans during our capture and in the Stalag. He told me that he had been working in Paris when civil war broke out in Spain. He and a friend decided that they would join the International Brigade and help the republicans repel the nationalist revolt.

I remembered that before Mary and I left for London, there had been a lot of talk in Ireland about the civil war that had broken out in Spain. The Church was an avid supporter of the nationalists, led by Franco, while there were some who believed that the duly elected republicans had right on their side. I had heard that Irish volunteers went to fight in the war for both the nationalists and the republicans.

'I don't understand. You told me some time ago that you are a Catholic, and yet you went to fight on the republican side. Were they not driven by the communists, and Franco's side were there as defenders of the Catholic faith?'

'Ah, if only life were so simple! Fascists have only one goal and that is the suppression of democracy. They will grind into the ground anyone who dares express a personal view. They use religion to camouflage their insidious objectives, while those at the top line their pockets with the spoils of the turmoil they have created. Yes, I am Catholic, but that does not mean that I do not also think and make decisions for myself. Life is a long road that leads to a crossroads. How you have travelled on that road will determine the turn that you will eventually take. Either up – or down,' he said, gesturing with his thumb.

'You are very profound, Krzysztof, and yes, I think you are right. I had no choice but to come and fight in this awful war. My father was coerced by his employers, who were aristocratic English landlords in Ireland, to fight for His Majesty against the Hun at the Somme. He also had little choice. Would we have done so voluntarily? I do not believe so because these are not our wars, but the consequences could have a detrimental impact on our lives. As you say – if only life were that simple.'

———

One night in early November, Krzysztof and I entered the Café Rivoli to find it almost empty, which was most unusual. As we walked past the marble counter behind which Pascal was busily shining glasses with a linen cloth, we could see four German officers and a young blonde girl, with whom they were engaged in flirtatious banter, seated at a table on the left of the room. One of the soldiers looked over at us with a wary glare. It was obvious that he had already had too much to drink. He called out and beckoned for us to come and sit with them.

We hesitantly shuffled towards the group when suddenly Odette emerged from behind the curtain separating the kitchen from the main room and began shouting at us to leave. Despite our feigned protests, she ushered us towards the door declaring that she had warned us the last time that we were not welcome in the café and that she would not tolerate the insolent behaviour that she had seen from us before.

The drunken officer stood up and objected, but his companions very quickly dragged him back to the table, where they resumed their frolicking. We then left as quickly as we could.

When we got back to Krzysztof's apartment, he said that it was unsafe for me to stay there as the *Boche* were all over the area. We then made the decision that I would have to leave as soon as possible. The next day, Krzysztof arranged for me to move to a small apartment owned by a French sympathiser on Rue Charlemagne, which was not far from Sully-Morland. I stayed there for three weeks until early December, when Hélène returned. She said that the plan for Marseilles had been abandoned because some of the Resistance leaders there had been compromised. Instead, I would follow the Comet Line and cross over the eastern side of the Pyrenees into Spain. The Comet Line was a contraband route over the Pyrenees used by smugglers. I was to leave the following day and take a train to Saint-Jean-de-Luz in south-western France. The journey would be risky, because this was to be my first time travelling without identity papers.

12.
A TASTE OF FREEDOM
DECEMBER 1942

Hélène came by early one morning. With her was a stocky Polish man named Mateusz. She gave me a train ticket for Saint-Jean-de-Luz, which she had bought the previous evening. I was to travel with Mateusz to the Spanish border and from there attempt entry into Spain via the Comet Line, and then on to Lisbon or Gibraltar. Since the papers I had were valid only as far as Dijon, I now found myself without identity documents, completely exposed.

Gare d'Austerlitz, on the left bank of the Seine, was only a short walk from the apartment where I had been holed up. The magnificent station, named after one of Napoleon's victorious battles, was relatively quiet and we were relieved that identity papers were not being looked for as we boarded the train.

The journey took over ten hours and our luck held out – there were no guards on board at any stage. It was early evening as the train rolled into the station at Saint-Jean-de-Luz. As passengers began to alight, Mateusz pulled at my elbow and indicated for me to follow behind the small crowd, but slowly.

As we cautiously moved along the platform, we spotted a security control up ahead at the exit gate.

On the other side of the platform, an empty train lay positioned in total darkness. Instinctively, we both moved closer to it. Mateusz reached out and tried the handle on one of the carriages. 'Damn!' he said as it failed to budge. He tried the next carriage, the same. But on the next, the door eased open. We looked around and up towards the guards. All was clear, as they were distracted checking passengers' papers. We heaved ourselves up the steps, gently closed the door and lay on our bellies under some seats. The stench in the dark compartment was a mixture of oil and dampness.

We waited and waited. After all had been silent in the station for some time, we decided to make our move. Looking through the grimy carriage window, we saw that the control post was unoccupied and there was no one around. We decided that it was safe to leave the carriage and tentatively climbed down again onto the platform. We hopped a low wooden fence beside the tracks and left the station.

Mateusz went into a café near the station and returned with a Basque man whom he introduced to me. He then left and I never saw him again. The Basque said his name was Patxi Gaztañaga. He gave me a beret and a pair of soft shoes that looked like slippers. We then left the café and walked for over six hours. At times we left the road and trudged across fields and streams until we reached a small farmhouse on the outskirts of a town called Urrugne.

Patxi knocked on that door and a friendly man and woman welcomed me into their home. Before leaving, Patxi said he would be back before dawn to get me. I was given a bowl of warm milk and an omelette with a chunk of bread. I could not understand a word they spoke in French, but their warmth gave me assurance that they wanted to help me. When it grew late, they indicated with hand signals that it was time for me to prepare to leave.

When Patxi returned, I thanked my hosts as best as I could and then we left the farmhouse and walked towards the foothills of the Pyrenees.

During our train journey, Mateusz had explained to me that a Basque smuggler would help me and show me a path over the mountains. He told me that there was a local network that had perfected its ability to move people and contraband goods in the dead of night. He said that, once in Spain, I should try to get to Bilbao or San Sebastián and make contact with the British consulate there. They had helped escapers before to get to the embassy in Madrid by hiding them in the boot of a car. Once in Madrid, they could arrange to transport them to Gibraltar.

The sky was heavy with clusters of constellations, and, from Big Bear, I could tell that we were heading south. As we set off, my guide warned me in very poor English that parts of the climb would be strenuous because of the icy conditions. He also told me to be on the lookout for any military patrols or wild animals. He said that bears and wolves could be seen from time to time in that area but his insistence that they were not dangerous unless they felt threatened did little to reassure me.

Luckily, I had recovered a considerable amount of my physical fitness since my escape from the Stalag, but the climb was extremely tough, compounded by the weather and the constant, searing pain from the piece of shrapnel embedded in my leg. A blustery wind swirled around us, stinging our faces with hailstones and ice blowing from the treetops.

The packed snow and ice underfoot made it difficult to walk. The cold penetrated my bones, reminding me of Poland, while the eerie silence was broken only by the rustling of branches and ferns as we dragged our feet upwards, step after step.

I prayed and hoped that this man knew where he was going. I was aware that the Nazis now occupied all of France and had patrols everywhere, particularly along the borders. At each turn that we took in the dim greyness, I half-expected to hear a Mauser being readily cocked. The sense of relief when that didn't happen allowed me the reward of a hearty exhalation of breath. Spain was now within reach.

After a gruelling climb, we reached the top of the mountain just as the sun's rays appeared over the horizon. Looking back, I'm sure it was a spectacular sunrise, but my mind was elsewhere at that moment and scenic views were not a priority.

At dawn, we stopped to rest for half an hour and Patxi gave me some bread and chocolate. Then he stretched out his arm and pointed down the mountain, nodding in the direction that I should follow. His rugged, weather-beaten face turned towards me, and his eyes looked forlornly into mine. Did he know something that he wasn't telling me? Mateusz had warned me that smugglers were not to be trusted and that it was not unusual for them to accept payment and, soon after, leave an escaper stranded in the wilderness, or worse. However, this man had so far proved to be honest and there was an air of humility and kindness about him. He had fulfilled his side of the deal and for that I was grateful and relieved.

We shook hands and he departed. I was now alone.

The freezing cold air of early morning cut through me. There was no time to stare at the deep valleys that lay below, shrouding my destiny in the overhanging mist.

As a boy back home, I used to run up and down the local hills with my friends, enjoying the sense of freedom that comes from delving into nature's treasures. But, in these circumstances, I could barely sense the magnitude of the beauty before me, my mind being preoccupied with what lay in store for me below.

For the first time since the night I had escaped from the Stalag, I found myself entirely on my own. I could hardly be more isolated than now, alone on top of the Pyrenees.

Well, Tommy boy, you're on top of the world! I said to myself.

In some ways, it felt like that. I thought back to the horrors of the camp, to the men who would desperately love to be where I was standing at that moment.

But it was time to begin my descent.

Step after step, I plodded on, my brain in a state of high alert, simultaneously engaged in watching the icy ground while looking out for hidden dangers. Patxi had told me that the Germans were constantly patrolling the mountains in search of any enemy, whether they were saboteurs or escaped prisoners of war. Every twig that cracked, every rock that moved caused my heart to jump. The sinews at the back of my neck felt as if they would tear apart with the tension.

With conditions so bad, I decided to shelter for a few hours. I found a crevice between some large rocks and squeezed my body through it. Stalactites hung from the hard rock, above which loomed the early morning sky.

I wondered what destiny awaited me. I thought back to Torun and my fellow captors. I could see Jim, Frank and the others lying in their bunks, twisting and turning, unable to sleep amidst the grunts and whimpers of others, the severe cold penetrating their very souls. At any moment, they would be dragged from their hard beds and made to line up to face another gruelling day of labour.

Well, Tommy, you've got this far. You've placed your bet. There's no going back, so just hope for the best! With my body shivering and my teeth chattering, I managed to doze a little. When I awoke, I eased myself out from between the rocks and continued my walk through the low-lying mist rising from the dewy ground.

Eventually, with my muscles aching and my stomach hurting, I saw the rooftops of two or three houses, smoke rising from their chimneys. The icy, rocky terrain then gave way to a mud path. As I approached the hamlet, I could see a number of loose dogs. They did not appear happy to see me. What to do? I thought about trying to go around the houses but concluded that that would be a waste of time as, undoubtedly, I would encounter exactly the same situation elsewhere.

You haven't gone through all that just to be defeated by some mutt grabbing you by the ankle, I said to myself. With a determined stride I proceeded to walk by the buildings.

The dogs went berserk.

I remembered Hopper, the old farmer outside of Portlaw, who had shown us a trick when we were children. I stopped in my tracks and turned. Staring the hounds in the eye, I stretched out my arm and shouted loudly. To my relief, it worked!

A door opened and a man looked out at me. I waved and kept going.

As I approached the town, I saw a medieval church with steep stone steps leading to its door. There I rested my exhausted body while I gathered my thoughts. The church was a beautiful Romanesque sandstone structure built on a higher level, overlooking the town hall and a large square. This was busy with people milling about here and there. I hardly saw them, my weary mind torn between jubilation at impending freedom and the dread of the unknown.

A huge sense of relief washed over me. A lump formed at the back of my throat. Here I was, finally in Spain. A country free from German occupation. *Could this be it?* I thought to myself. *Am I really free? Will I see Mary soon? And my family?* Everything looked so peaceful, so normal. *Oh God, thank you, thank you, I knew you'd help me. I knew you'd get me out.*

I sat there in the late afternoon with the fading sun casting its shadow over the rooftops, watching as small children played among the pillars in the alcoves of the town hall. Old men in berets sat at tables outside a decrepit bar, drinking Basque liqueurs and brandies. Some were engrossed in a game of cards while others engaged in what looked at a distance to be serious conversations. Young mothers walked side by side, pushing prams and exchanging pleasantries. Older women huddled together, some in black shawls, their heads nodding as they talked.

My mind drifted back to when I was a child growing up in Portlaw, a similar-sized village to this. We used to play all sorts of games like these, but one that I particularly loved, especially when I was very small, was hide-and-seek. The thought then struck me, how ironic, that I was still playing hide-and-seek now!

A hazy shape at the far end of the square began to come into focus as it approached. It was the three-cornered hat that first caught my attention. And the rifle over the Guardia Civil's shoulder made me sit up.

13.

INTERNMENT
DECEMBER 1942–APRIL 1943

The Guardia Civil sergeant in charge of the station, seeing me staring at the blue Celtic warrior on the crumpled packet of Celtas cigarettes on the table between us, reached down and slowly raised the pack to offer me one. I took it and used the match that he gave me to light it. The tobacco seared the back of my throat as the heady smoke filled my lungs. 'Thank you,' I said.

The sergeant sat across the table from me. His upper lip was graced with a dark, bushy moustache, speckled with hints of grey. His round glasses were slightly smudged and partially hid the weary eyes that studied me. He continued to do so for what seemed like an age. Eventually, he extinguished his cigarette in an ashtray made of shell and resignedly shook his head.

Earlier, the younger Guardia Civil who arrested me had asked me for my papers at the church. When I could produce none, he unshouldered his rifle and, prodding my back with it, marched me to the Guardia Civil station.

After some time, when it was clear that I could not speak Spanish or Basque, the sergeant decided that he could not deal with me so would refer the matter to a higher authority. I was then taken to another building and placed in a cell on my own.

I discovered that the name of the town was Bera. It was situated on the River Bidasoa and, from what I had seen, it appeared to have survived the civil war unscathed. Through rusty iron bars on the window, I could see tree branches swaying in the wind. I could hear birds chirping over the distant rumble of small-town life outside. Was this to be my new dwelling?

For Christ's sake, what the hell am I doing here? First, I got dragged into a war that my own country was not even fighting, and now here I am, locked up again in another country, not knowing anyone, not being able to speak with anyone. How much more, dear God? How much more? My muscles ached from the climb over the mountains. My feet were in bits, blood-filled blisters making it difficult to walk without excruciating pain. My shrapnel wound was throbbing. Whatever euphoria I had felt earlier had by now evaporated. I drifted off into an uneasy slumber.

Later that evening, the cell door opened, and a guard beckoned me out. I followed him along a narrow corridor and soon found myself in a smoke-filled room. A yellow bulb hanging from the ceiling provided some dim lighting. The sergeant from earlier was standing beside a desk. Beside him was a woman sitting on a chair. A dark-skinned man in uniform sitting behind the desk indicated for me to come forward. He was younger than the sergeant. A pencil-thin black moustache complemented his slick black hair. His shiny three-cornered hat rested on the table beside his elbow.

He said something in Spanish to the woman, who then turned to me.

'My name is Harriet Rankin. I'm here to translate for you and these gentlemen,' she said in a pronounced American accent.

With Harriet's help, I answered the police officer's questions. I told him of my captivity in Poland and my subsequent escape. I went on to tell him how I had crossed the Pyrenees and how it had been my intention to get to Gibraltar and so return to England. I made great emphasis of the fact that I was Irish, and said that, like Spain, Ireland was also a neutral country.

The officer pushed back his chair and eased himself upright. He walked to the window with his hands crossed behind his back. He turned and said something that I did not understand, but from the tone, I knew it was not good news for me.

The interpreter said that he was more or less complaining that he was fed up with foreigners coming to Spain. He said that they had had to put up with many of them who had fought in the civil war against Franco, but that they had lost. She emphasised the glee in the officer's tone when recounting this part. He wanted to see no more intruders come into his country and the fact that I had done so without any identity papers left him with no choice but to imprison me. With that, he saluted his subordinate and left the room.

Harriet got up to leave and shook my hand. She told me not to despair, that she would notify the British consulate in Bilbao about my case. I thanked her, but at that moment, her words gave me little assurance or comfort.

On 10 December, I was moved to a prison in nearby Irun. The British consul made arrangements for me to get food from outside because the prison diet was appalling and the rations abysmal. I shared a cell with two local Spaniards. One was still so drunk that I could not imagine what crime he would have been capable of committing in his condition. I later found out that the other man was from Irun and was suspected of having supported the republican cause in the civil war. Neither spoke any English. We each had a blanket to cover us to sleep on the hard wooden floor. An open hole in the ground in the cell was our toilet.

I knew all the risks that I was taking the minute I climbed over that wall in Torun. Being shot was obviously number one. Being captured and thrown in jail in Spain had never been on my list.

On 16 December, I was transferred to the concentration camp at Miranda de Ebro. The train journey through northern Spain took just under six hours.

The camp was located just beside the railway station on the outskirts of the town. As I descended from our carriage in the crisp morning air, I could see the rooftops of hundreds of white concrete bunkers, built side by side along a vast open space, surrounded by concrete walls. At each corner, there stood a watch tower with an armed guard vigilantly watching over the area.

I was marched the short distance to the main gate. Once

inside, I could see that the camp was teeming with men, some just loitering, others sitting idly, while many stood over a large laundry area, washing clothes, their sleeves rolled up and their backs bent.

I was taken to a whitewashed building, where I was told to sit and wait. A short time later a soldier came to escort me into a room. Inside were a table and two chairs. He sat down on one and pointed for me to sit on the other chair opposite him.

He spoke reasonably good English and produced a few sheets of blank paper, then began to ask me questions, to which he wrote down my answers in Spanish. He asked me where I had come from and what my background was. I told him that I was Irish but that I had been living and working in London when war broke out and that I had been conscripted into the army. I explained how I had been captured and I gave him details of my escape. He produced the aluminium tag with my POW number on it, which had been taken from me in Bera. He asked me what it was. I explained that in the Stalag we were all given one of these tags with our own number. I had decided to carry it with me in case I was caught. I felt that I might stand a better chance of not being shot if I could prove that I was not a spy. He wrote down every detail of my journey since leaving the Stalag – my travels through Berlin, Paris, and across the Pyrenees. He noted that I had done so without a guide, a map or a compass. When he asked me for information about those who had helped me along the way, I repeatedly refused to respond. At the end, he asked me to sign the document, which I did.

I was issued with a tin plate and cup, a cotton pair of trousers, and a flimsy jacket with the letter 'P' sewn onto it. I was taken to one of the small huts and given a thin, ragged blanket and a bundle of straw on which I was to sleep on the concrete floor. There was no glass in the small windows and there was no heating of any kind.

Over the next few days, I settled into my new life, not knowing if or when I would ever be free. It did not take me long to see that some of the prisoners were treated more harshly than others. There were nearly five thousand prisoners being held in a camp that was built to hold just fifteen hundred. We were woken each morning with a bugle call at 6.30 a.m., and the guards would tear through each hut, using whips on those who struggled to get to their feet promptly. The food rations were made up of either watery cabbage soup or greasy potatoes.

Just like at the Stalag, lice infestation was rampant. It tormented men who could not stop themselves from intensely scratching, which in many cases resulted in developing scabies. There were twenty taps over a common basin and a dozen showers, many of them broken. It was nearly impossible to keep oneself clean.

Dysentery was also rife. The men continued to complain of the cold, but for me, after Poland, it was not too bad. The weather was the least of my worries. Instead, I would despondently ponder, *where has my life gone?* An unthinkable series of events that had visited me these past few years made me wonder what more I must go through. Would I have been better off as one of those poor lads who had been slaughtered on the fields of France? Their distorted faces with pained looks of utter shock are seared into my consciousness for all time. The trauma of experiencing our rescue being torn from our grasp on the beach at Saint-Valery. Our capture and our terrible humiliation. The suffering we endured through our forced march across France, Belgium, and into Holland, without knowing what our destiny was to be. The psychological pain was worse than the agonising rifle blows from our guards and our lacerated, blistered feet. And then, the years of confinement in the Stalag, and hunger like I had never imagined. I took my chance in escaping. I knew the risks and decided to do it. But, to come to this, no! A prisoner once again. This time in a supposedly neutral country, but that didn't seem to make any difference. Was all that I had been through futile? Was this how it would end? And why had I not heard anything from the British consulate? Surely they hadn't forgotten me.

————

There were many nationalities in the camp. I came to learn that these were the men who had travelled to Spain to join the international brigades on the side of the republicans against Franco's nationalists. Franco had won the civil war in 1939, yet these men and their Spanish comrades were still being held in captivity four years later. With the fall of Vichy France in November 1942, conditions in the camp had improved somewhat.

I became friendly with an American who had come to Spain to, in his words, 'help to stop the curse of fascism'. His name was George. Over a period of weeks, George and some of his friends enlightened me on what had gone on in Spain and in the camp. Those whom I had witnessed being badly treated were former republican soldiers. I was told that up until recently they had been held in shackles and were beaten regularly.

In the early years of the camp, which was built in 1937 to cater for republican prisoners, horrible atrocities had been carried out, with special attention being given to Basque priests, who were repeatedly derided, humiliated and occasionally tortured for being sympathetic to the republican cause. Even though conditions in the camp continued to be poor, I was told that the death rate from malnutrition and disease had substantially decreased in recent times.

From early 1942, when Franco saw the tide turn against the Axis powers in the war, he decided to distance himself from Hitler and Mussolini. He even stopped the Gestapo from continuing their regular visits to the camp, though they had helped design it in the first place. I thanked my lucky stars for my good fortune. If I had ended up at the camp some months earlier, I would have undoubtedly been sent back to Germany – and have had to face the consequences.

———

In early April 1943, I received a visit from an emissary from the British consulate in Bilbao, James Caplin. Mr Caplin introduced himself, assured me that I had not been forgotten, and added that every effort was being made to secure my release as soon as possible.

At that point I could no longer contain my frustration. 'Well, that is good to hear, Mr Caplin, but I've been in this godforsaken hole now for five months. This on top of what I've been through the past four years for a king and country that is not even mine. Isn't Spain neutral? Why am I being held here at all? Surely you can provide me with something to show them so that they set me free. Do I have to risk my life again and try and escape?'

'I know, Corporal, that it has been very hard.'

'You know damn all, Mr Consul. You haven't one idea what I have been through. You haven't any idea of what my friends still lying rotting in Poland are going through.

And we were the lucky ones – at least we didn't get killed or have our legs blown off. Do you know what it's like to see a man trying to hold in his guts with his bare hands and see the expression of incredulity and shock on his face while the blood drains from his veins? Or innocent women and children torn to shreds while their limbs are scattered along the wayside? No, Mr Caplin, I'm afraid you do not know.'

'I'm so sorry, Tommy, I really am,' the consul replied. 'And it's not just talk when I say that. Yes, we are doing everything we can for you. A number of Allied embassies are putting pressure on Franco to release all Allied personnel held in camps throughout Spain. They are threatening to cut off supplies of raw materials and it seems to be working. Now that Franco sees that the Germans are on the retreat, he is doing his utmost to cosy up to Britain and the United States. So, hang on a little while longer. I promise you that it won't be long, and we'll get you back home.'

'I hope so, Mr Caplin. I don't know how much more of this I can take. Forgive my outburst, but I need to do something to get out of here.'

In the end, we shook hands and I thanked him warmly for rekindling the spark in my soul.

A week later, another agent of the British consul came to see me. He stayed for only a moment and told me, 'In two days you must start to complain of severe stomach pain. Keep this up and, on the following day, Mr Caplin will come.'

He would say no more and left as abruptly as he had come.

Two days later, on the morning of 14 April, I called one of the guards and told him that I was suffering severe stomach pains. I was brought to an area that acted as a field infirmary. Rows of beds lined the walls of a large, high-roofed room. The warm air was putrid, with a mixture of odours of human waste and antiseptic disinfectant. I lay in a bed staring at the ceiling wondering what would happen next. What had Mr Caplin in store for me?

One day later, I was handed into the care of Mr Caplin and left the concentration camp at Miranda de Ebro. As the car drove out of the gates of the camp, I had to pinch myself to make sure that this was really happening. But what lay ahead? God only knew! At this stage of my journey, nothing surprised me any longer. The main thing was that I was out of that hellhole and now I began to think I might just make it after all. My spirits were up and the farther we drove on through the undulating countryside and away from the camp, the better I began to feel.

14.

FREEDOM AT LAST
APRIL 1943

Although it was still early spring, the sun's rays shimmered off the black car's bonnet. Golden sunflowers danced in the fields as we wound our way through the Meseta, the heartland of Spain. I was in high spirits.

'Tell me, Caplin, how on earth did you manage to swing that one? Surely they must have known what was going on?'

'Oh, they knew alright. You see, it's all part of a game. Franco wants to hedge his bets now that the German Army is on the back foot. They suffered enormous losses in Stalingrad and that has changed everything. The Gestapo has had a huge influence in overseeing the camp in Miranda and the Spaniards cannot be seen to be helping any Allied prisoners. So what do they do? They turn a blind eye. They knew very well that there was nothing wrong with you, yet they still released you specifically to us to get proper medical care.'

'Thank God for my timing! Can you imagine if I had arrived there a year earlier?'

'I have no doubt. You would have been handed straight over to the Gestapo, who would have executed you in the blink of an eye. So relax, old boy – all is good!'

I began to believe that I was actually going to make it.

We drove through the medieval city of Burgos, which had been a hotbed of Franco's nationalist rebellion during the civil war, and whose many buildings lay in ruins. As we continued our southerly journey, I was captivated by the beauty and enormity of the desert plains. I had never before seen such a landscape.

We stopped in the town of Aranda de Duero to get some rest. The poverty was appalling, and emaciated children flocked around us, seeking something to eat. A local woman threw them some biscuits, which they devoured ferociously. The poor children and their parents had been through such horrendous hardship for over three years in the recent civil war in which half a million souls had perished. Their lives had been torn asunder, left with little food and their homes destroyed.

———

Five hours later we approached the outskirts of Madrid, the enormous metropolis first coming into view as we turned a bend. Driving down the broad Castellana Avenida, we entered the very heart of the city. The streets were bustling with trams, buses and cars. It was late afternoon, shortly after siesta, and people went about their business as usual. If it wasn't for the bombed-out buildings and strong military presence, I would never have known that these very streets had only recently been torn apart in a horrendous and bloody civil war where brother fought against brother and friend against friend.

Fernando el Santo was a narrow tree-lined street off the main Castellana Avenue. The Union Jack fluttered over the large mahogany doors of the British embassy. Mr Caplin and

I were met by a friendly young Englishman and shown into a wood-panelled room adorned with portraits and dotted with leather armchairs. A photograph of King George VI rested on the mantelpiece of the unlit fireplace.

I heard footsteps approaching from the hall and two men entered the room. The older man was immaculately dressed in a suit and silk tie. The silver colour of his tie matched his well-groomed hair. The younger man was tall, with strong features and jet-black hair. He wore silver-rimmed glasses, which rested halfway down his nose. We stood up immediately.

Addressing the older man, Caplin said, 'Sir, this is Corporal McGrath.' Turning his head towards me, he continued, 'Corporal, this is His Excellency Samuel Hoare, 1st Viscount Templewood, the British ambassador.'

I approached and shook the ambassador's outstretched hand.

'Well done, corporal, I've been told your story. Quite remarkable, really! Now, don't worry, we'll get you back home safely soon enough. Let me introduce you to Hugh Pollard,' he said, gesturing to the man at his side. 'Hugh is MI6. No doubt you two will have a lot to talk about.'

I said that I was pleased to meet Pollard and then thanked them for rescuing me from the concentration camp at Miranda.

'You're a lucky son of a gun, McGrath. A year ago and I'm afraid we could have done nothing for you.'

'I know, sir. I understand.'

'Mr Caplin will take you now to a safe house, not far away. It's a *pensión*, but it's run by a friendly old man and his wife, with whom we have an understanding. Have a good night's rest. I want to see you back here in the morning at ten. We have many matters to discuss.'

Caplin and I left the embassy. After a twenty-minute walk we arrived at the *pensión* in Calle Fernando el Católico. Caplin accompanied me up the steps and introduced me to the owners. He suggested that I have a shower and rest and that he would be back for me in two hours so we could go for a meal.

The steaming hot water eased my weary body, seeming to wash away all my aches through my open pores. The horrors and trials I had witnessed somehow eased from my body, though I knew that they would remain in my inner being for ever more. I still could not quell the constant fear that at any moment I might find myself face to face with the enemy pointing a Luger at me.

A little while later, feeling more rested than I had in months, I dressed and walked down the stairs to wait for Caplin. A young couple passed me in the hallway holding hands. He was tall and balding, and she was petite and dark. They smiled at me as we passed. It struck me that amidst all the carnage that had recently been visited on this poor country, life went on and people still fell in love.

Caplin arrived and we walked for about twenty minutes to a restaurant called Casa Botín, where he treated me to a meal. It was a very old establishment with wood-panelled walls, marble-topped tables and large mahogany rafters supporting the high ceiling. The cured ham and roasted lamb cutlets together with fresh bread were delicious. I never could have imagined in my wildest dreams while in the Stalag that I would ever enjoy such a feast.

Amidst the chatter and clanging of plates and cutlery in the smoked-filled room, we proceeded to devour and relish the tasty dishes presented to us. We exchanged pleasantries and information on our experiences.

Over coffee, the conversation returned to the topic of my capture and escape.

'It must have been rough in France; I've heard the conditions were atrocious.'

I looked Caplin in the eye for a moment, then looked to the ceiling to contemplate my reply.

'We were sheep sent to slaughter. How on earth did they think we could stand up to the Germans with the rubbish we had for arms? I mean, they were the same rifles my father used in the Great War. And I'll tell you, the Nazis came at us with new and modern artillery that we had no chance against.'

Caplin raised himself in the chair and said, 'Yes, well, don't forget we went through the Great Depression in the thirties and as well as that of course, the Germans were forbidden by the Versailles Treaty to increase their army stockpiles.'

'Now where have I heard that before? So much for treaties,' I replied.

'So much for Hitler, Tommy, so much for Hitler,' sighed Caplin.

As we finished our meal and Caplin was paying the bill, I said, 'You know, Caplin, this is just incredible. I have never eaten so well.'

'I'm delighted, old boy. You well deserve it.'

'But something's niggling me. I can't help thinking about the men I left behind. I can't stop imagining what they are going through. I'm torn apart.'

'You say that as though you have a sense of guilt. Do you?'

'I don't really know. It's funny, but I feel as if I belong back there with them.'

'You have nothing to feel guilty about. You had the balls to get out and escape. That was your choice; you took the risk. It was open to others to do the same. They chose not to. You took your opportunity and made it work. For that, you should feel happy and proud.'

'Oh, I am very happy, believe me. I'm not sure that pride enters into it, and I certainly don't think it's a question of balls. I left many men behind who were far braver than me, but who, for whatever reason, decided to bide their time. Perhaps they have families with children and thought better of taking such a risk. And then, of course, there are the poor sods who are too injured to even think about escaping. No, the fact is I took a chance and luck was on my side. If it hadn't been for the kindness and bravery of the Resistance, I wouldn't have got very far, starting with the old Pole who opened the door of his little house in the woods.' I raised my glass of wine. 'To the Resistance!' Our glasses chimed as they clinked.

After dinner, Caplin walked with me to my *pensión*. I assured him that I could find my way back to the embassy the following morning. He said that he was leaving early the next day to return to Bilbao. I thanked him for everything that he and his colleagues had done. We said our goodbyes and he turned and walked away into the darkness.

It was still early and, although I was quite tired, the exhilaration of the day's events had my nerves on fire with adrenaline. I decided to go for a stroll.

I wandered down Castellana Avenue. The bars were thronged with people eating and drinking. Clusters of men and women made their way down the streets. It was as if there had been a gigantic sigh of relief that the war was over, and everyone was doing everything possible to get back to normality. After soaking up enough atmosphere for one night, I decided to return to the *pensión*. When I reached the front door, to my shock it was locked. I later learned that it was the norm in Spain for all front doors of buildings to close at 10 p.m. for security. There was no bell, or anything to knock with. All I could do was wait for another guest of the *pensión* to come along.

After about an hour, an elderly man approached. I was sure that he was heading for my door, but at the last second he took a key from his pocket and moved towards the adjoining doorway. I walked over to him and from my gestures, he immediately understood my predicament.

He raised his hand in a calming gesture as if to tell me not to worry. He then joined his two hands together and began clapping loudly. He continued at this for some minutes until there appeared a rather rotund figure in a long overcoat with a ring full of keys dangling from his belt.

My new neighbour smiled at me and giggled. '*Sereno, sereno,*' he said. He then held up his hand to indicate the number five with his fingers and repeated, '*Pesetas, pesetas.*'

I knew that he was telling me that I should give this night watchman a tip of five pesetas. Fortunately, Caplin had handed me the change from the meal in the restaurant, in case I would need it. I wondered if he had foreseen my little adventure.

———

The following morning I presented myself at the embassy and met Mr Pollard.

He brought me to a room overlooking the leafy street. The early sunlight poured through the open windows, filling the room with warmth.

Looking down his nose through his steel-rimmed spectacles, Mr Pollard began to question me in detail about everything that had happened since my arrival in France with the BEF three years before. He took copious notes and when we were finished, he thanked me. He said that when I got back to London I would be interviewed again by a number of agencies because it was important to find out as much as possible about the enemy. I told him that I would be glad to assist, although I don't think I really had much choice in the matter.

As I got up to leave, I said, 'I wonder if I could ask a huge favour of you. Would it be possible for me to call my wife and family to let them know that I'm alright?'

'While I would love to help you, old chap, and I understand your eagerness, I am afraid that any call by you to the UK from Spain would be out of the question. However, I'll see what else I can do. Just write out your family's names and addresses before you leave.'

I thanked him, wrote out the details and left.

—————

I spent eight days in Madrid. On the seventh day, I was called to the embassy, where I was told that the following day I would be brought to Gibraltar, from where I would take a boat back to Scotland. I could not believe what I was hearing. A huge wave of emotion engulfed me. At last! It was finally happening. I was going home, leaving all the terror and pain behind. Now, what would I find when I got back? Would Mary be alright? What if she was not there? How bad had the bombings been? Would I be treated as a coward for having allowed myself to be captured? My mind began to swirl. It was some time before I could compose myself enough to leave the building.

15.

THE RETURN
APRIL 1943

After I arrived in Gibraltar, two days before my departure for Scotland, I was examined by a doctor and underwent a barrage of tests. My wounds from the explosion were looked at and I was told that I would have to live with the shrapnel in my leg for the rest of my life. That did not really bother me once I got assurance that it would not cause me any serious problems apart from some pain every now and then. I enjoyed a lengthy sulphur bath to eradicate any remaining lice. I was also given a haircut, a fresh uniform, and managed to have a good rest for a whole day.

The consul told me that I was to be ferried home on a merchant ship carrying supplies between the UK and Gibraltar. The ships travelled in convoy so as to provide protection for each other in the event of an attack by German U-boats, which trawled the seabed of the Atlantic. The RAF would provide limited cover, but there was always the risk of attack and many ships on the route had been sunk.

As I boarded the merchant ship that formed part of the convoy that would bring me back to Britain, I took one last look at the landscape of Gibraltar and the coastline of the Iberian Peninsula. When we cast off, it felt as if the chains that bound me for the previous three years were being shed.

As I lay on my bunk, I thought about my family in Ireland – and about Mary. I had asked the embassy if they could get word to her that I was coming home. I could hardly contain my excitement and was hoping Mary could let everybody back in Portlaw know that I would soon return.

————

We docked early on the morning of 30 April. The ship had taken seven days to reach Gourock, the port of Glasgow. I then made my way to Glasgow Central Station, from where I would catch a train to London. Having survived the horrors of a prisoner-of-war camp, followed by over a year of surviving on my wits to avoid recapture and execution, I was finally back in familiar territory.

Before boarding the train, I found a phone box and dialled the number of the Maxwells' home. Mrs Maxwell answered after a few rings.

'Mrs Maxwell, it's me, Tommy McGrath,' I said breathlessly. 'I'm back home. Well, not exactly – I'm in Glasgow waiting for a train to London. Is Mary there?'

'Oh Tommy, thank goodness you're safe! We thought we'd never see you again. Oh, I'm so happy.'

'Thank you, ma'am. Yes, I'm very glad to be back. I was wondering if Mary was in.'

'No, Tommy, I'm afraid that Mary no longer lives here. She left a couple of years ago to take up work in a hotel in central London. She will be so relieved to hear you are safe.'

'Did you not get a call from Spain to tell Mary I was okay?'

'No, Tommy, we never heard a word.'

'Would you know which hotel she now works at, ma'am?'

'Off the top of my head I can't remember, but she did ask me for a reference and the hotel manager did call to check it out. I took a note of it, I know. I'll have to look for it and hope I can find it. Can you call me back?'

'I will, ma'am, but it will be tomorrow, if that's alright. I have to return to register at the barracks today.'

'Yes, of course, Tommy. I'll see what I can do.'

———

I arrived at Euston Station in the early hours of the following morning and took the Tube to Waterloo Station. From there I boarded a train to Aldershot. I was met by a driver and taken to the office of Lieutenant Colonel Brookes, who greeted me warmly. He was middle-aged, with the appearance of a school headmaster. He had silver-grey hair, which crowned a round head, with solid features and deep-brown eyes.

He asked me to tell him of my experiences.

In great detail I told him of our battle engagements with the enemy when they broke through the Ardennes by surprise. I described the atrocious fighting we had endured in our retreat to Saint-Valery-en-Caux, the long march to

Holland in inhumane conditions and, finally, my experience in the Stalag and eventual escape.

The lieutenant colonel got up from his chair, pushed it back and walked slowly around to where I was sitting. He stood behind me and, placing a hand on my shoulder, leaned over and said, 'Son, I mean tell me about your real experience.'

He then walked back and sat down again. He took up a packet of cigarettes and offered me one. I took one and lit it with a lighter on the desk. He raised an eyebrow, an expression that seemed to say, 'Well?'

'It was awful, sir, just awful. The bitter fighting that broke out as we engaged the Germans in our retreat to the coast was horrific. I saw men being blown to pieces as they stood beside me, their limbs doing somersaults in the air before landing in a ditch or in the mud. Friends, who only a few hours before had sat with me in a trench waiting for dawn, were mowed down before my eyes, some with bayonets thrust into their bellies, ripping their intestines apart. The raised hopes of an evacuation that never materialised served only to demoralise our spirits even further. Some men jumped from the cliff edge, only to crash on the jagged rocks below, rather than risk being taken by the surrounding enemy. And then, the final humiliation of capture. We were shattered, utterly exhausted and beaten. We could not believe it. They forced us to march for three long weeks. The guards were savages.

If we slowed or stopped to tend to our bleeding blisters, a blow from the butt of a rifle or a prod of a bayonet in the back compelled us to keep going, despite the agonising pain.

'I've told you of the unspeakable conditions in the Stalag and of the inhumane treatment we received. It got to us all, some more than others. I know of some men who committed suicide. Others just went insane before our eyes. I had to get out. I could not endure any more. Once I had made that decision, I spent several months planning how I would do it and preparing for when the right time came.

'Sure, I took a chance, but I felt it was worth it. The future in the Stalag was unknown and we had heard some stories of Nazi atrocities happening in other camps, so once I had made the decision, that was it. The rest was up to me to do the best I could and pray for a little luck. Fortunately, I had quite a lot of luck, starting with the first house I came upon. With respect, sir, you have no idea of the valuable work the Resistance is doing.'

'I understand, Tommy – carry on.'

'I had a lot of near misses along the way and being stopped by the enemy when you are carrying false papers can be quite an experience, I assure you,' I said with a half-smile. 'Surprisingly, one of the most difficult things for me to overcome was the lack of companionship. What I mean is, I missed having people around me whom I knew and could trust. Sure, I got to know some of those in the Resistance who risked their lives to help me and we got on well, but even in a crowd I was on the lookout, always on guard to see who would reach for a pistol.

'I would often stay locked away all day wherever I was hiding. It is amazing the sounds that we take for granted. I longed to hear the birds chirping, the creaking of children's swings and laughter, or the sound of a gushing waterfall. I suppose I must thank my lucky stars that I will soon have all that back again. My biggest sorrow is when I think of the lads in the Stalag and what they're still going through. Is there much hope of getting them back soon, sir?'

'Well yes, there is, Tommy. The war is changing and now, with American support, it's only a matter of time. I can say no more than that, you understand.'

'Of course, sir.'

'That is quite a story, my man. You did your regiment proud. It will take you some weeks to recover, we understand that. Tomorrow you will be interviewed by MI5 and MI6 and the Yanks want to talk to you the following day. Just tell them all that you have told me and you'll be fine. So for now, that's all. Dismissed, corporal.'

The lieutenant colonel stood up and walked me to the door. As we reached it, I said, 'Excuse me, sir, may I ask you a question?'

'Yes, go ahead.'

'Well, sir, there was a general feeling among us all that

the 51st Regiment was sacrificed to drum up French eagerness to fight and resist surrender. We were aware that Major General Fortune had asked for permission to retreat because of the poor state of the French but that it was refused. That was three full weeks before we were eventually captured. Enough time for us to have been evacuated at Dunkirk with the rest of the BEF.'

'I'm afraid, corporal, that that feeling was ill-informed. Your regiment was sent to the Maginot Line three weeks before the present government took office. Yes, it was sent to beef up the French with reinforcements, but you will also be aware that the Maginot Line is more than two hundred miles from the English Channel. No one expected the German panzers to break through the Ardennes in the north, thereby cutting off your regiment from the rest of the BEF. And that is the simple reason why you didn't make it to Dunkirk. Furthermore, when you did eventually get to the coast at Saint-Valery-en-Caux, a mini flotilla of two hundred small boats, along with the Royal Navy, did sail but had to abandon at the last minute because of the weather.

'What happened in northern France was nothing short of a miracle. We still do not know exactly why Hitler halted the advance of his troops, which, had they continued, would have undoubtedly wiped out practically all the BEF. I'm afraid, it was just pure bad luck that the 51st were where they were at the time.'

With that I thanked him. We saluted one another and shook hands.

Later that evening, I asked for permission to make a local phone call. Once again, Mrs Maxwell answered. She told me that she had found the note where she had scribbled the name of the hotel. It was Bailey's Hotel, Gloucester Road, South Kensington, London SW7. I thanked her and told her how very grateful I was for the way that she and Dr Maxwell had so kindly treated us and also for looking after Mary while she was alone.

———

On May Day 1943, I was interviewed for a number of hours by both MI5 and MI6 at their offices in Vauxhall. Over the coming days, an American officer also interrogated me in great depth, wanting to know every detail of what I had found out about the Germans. After each interview, I was asked to read the statement that had been compiled and then sign it.

The last interview was with the adjutant general, a very senior officer whose job it was to oversee the welfare of soldiers. Once again, I told my story and once again copious notes were taken, only this time I was not asked to sign a statement at the end. The general, whose name I forget, said that he was there for any help I might need. He told me that I was being granted ten days' leave, after which I was to report back to Aldershot where I would be reassigned to a new regiment. He thanked me for my cooperation, and I left.

It was late afternoon when I decided to take the underground to Gloucester Road. Bailey's Hotel was just across the road from the Tube station. I decided that the best thing for me to do was to go straight to the reception desk in the hotel. I entered the plush lobby of the swanky hotel, the likes of which I had never seen before. I approached a young lady behind the shiny, dark mahogany desk and told her that I was Mary McGrath's husband and that I had been away and was trying to locate her. She told me that she would check and went off into a back office.

I was so nervous expecting Mary to walk out at any moment. What would happen? Would she rush into my open arms and kiss me like we used to do? Supposing she had changed? Maybe the war had affected her somehow, or maybe she had gone back home to Ireland? No – not my Mary.

After a while, the young lady came back and told me that Mary had left for the day but that she would be back the following morning at eight. She said that she was not permitted to give me Mary's home address. I said that I understood, thanked her and left. I returned to barracks and decided that I would go back to Gloucester Road in the morning.

I knew that Mary would probably arrive ten or fifteen

minutes before eight, so I made sure to arrive at half-past seven. I went into the hotel and asked if I could speak with the manager. When a smartly dressed man in his fifties arrived at the lobby, I told him who I was. I explained that Mary was going to be in shock when she saw me and asked for his understanding and compassion. He smiled warmly and, to my delight, he said that of course he understood. He suggested that Mary could take the morning off if she was not up to finishing her shift. I thanked him profusely and went outside, where I waited until Mary arrived.

She approached the hotel at around ten minutes to eight. At first, she did not see me, but as she got nearer I could see the look of disbelief and confusion in her eyes. She staggered and leaned a hand against a wall to steady herself. She was about to faint when I grabbed her.

'Mary, Mary! It's me, Tommy. I'm back.'

She looked up at me, but her eyes did not see me. It was as if I was invisible and all she could see was the wall behind me. Then her eyes filled with tears.

'Come, come, we'll go in here,' I said as I guided her inside a small café. The bare shelves above the counter underlined the effects of food rationing. Yet the imaginative staff had managed to rustle up some breakfast, albeit spartan, for the half a dozen or so customers seated around the room. There was a gentle murmur in the air as some caught up with the latest news from the front with the morning newspapers.

Minutes passed. Eventually, her sobbing subsided and Mary wiped the tears from her eyes, which were now bright red. The waitress brought us two cups of tepid coffee made from chicory. She looked at Mary quizzically, then turned to me and asked, 'She alright then, guv?'

'Yes, she's fine, thank you.' She nodded and walked away.

'I thought you were dead, Tommy. We read how you'd been surrounded by the Germans. We never, ever thought you'd survive. It's been three years. Oh Tommy, what have I done? Oh, holy Jesus, what have I done?'

'It's alright, Mary, I'm back now and —'

'No, no, Tommy, it's not alright,' she said, her sobs redoubling. 'You were dead. You were gone. I was on my own ... oh, Tommy, Tommy, how can I say it? How can I tell you? I met another man, and I've been living with him now for nearly two years.'

Shock is a funny thing. You don't realise what it is until it passes. When it starts, it catapults you into a state of nonchalance. Your senses become numb. Noise becomes a buzzing and vision a blur. What seems a lifetime passes in a matter of moments. And then you are catapulted into raw reality.

'I see,' I said slowly, although I clearly didn't. 'What do you want to do?'

'Oh Tommy, please try to understand! You were never coming back. I've moved on with my life. I know this must be such a horrible moment for you, but —'

'But I did come back!'

'I'm so sorry, Tommy, I really am.'

Without a further word being said, I knew there and then that our marriage was over. I felt hollow. How could this be happening? Rage engulfed me. All the pain and suffering I had been through – had it all been for nothing? It took every ounce of self-control to stop myself from screaming.

We sat in silence for what felt like over an hour. Then we stood up and walked out into the busy street. I put my arms around Mary and we hugged as tears rolled down both our cheeks. Her skin felt soft against mine while the scent of her perfume only added fuel to the flames in my heart. A wisp of her hair reminded me of close moments that were now gone for ever. Our silent sobbing played witness to the ebbing tide of our relationship. I kissed her one last time, and I then left.

The next day, I took a train to Holyhead, from where I caught the mail boat back to Dublin. I had to remind myself every now and then to relax. There weren't going to be any guards looking to check my papers. Apart from the real threat of U-boats, all was well and I arrived safely in Dún Laoghaire in the early morning.

I made my way to Kingsbridge Station and boarded a train to Waterford. I took delight in seeing the faces of ordinary Irish people, who were oblivious, by and large, of the horrors being inflicted in battlefields far away. At Waterford Station I was met by two of my brothers, Jamesie and Willie, whom I had sent a telegram to the day before. I was safe. I felt content. I was home at last.

In the bus on the way home, Jamesie gently explained that our father had passed away three years before, when I was in France with the BEF. They had had no idea of where to find me to let me know. The news hit me like a bolt of lightning. At that moment, my mind and heart were being pulled in every direction. My poor, poor Daddy. He had worked so hard all his life. He made me the man I was.

We arrived in Portlaw, where my other brothers and sisters had come to the bus stop to greet me. We hugged and cried, overcome with emotion, and made our way through the village and over the bridge to Coolfin, which was just on the outskirts. Neighbours spilled out from half-doors and cheered as I passed by.

When I reached the door of the house, I sensed a familiar comforting warmth envelop me. I opened the latch on the door and entered alone. The hall was as I remembered it, with the same beige flowered wallpaper. The living room was to the left. Its door was open, and I could see the flicker of flames in the fireplace reflecting on the wall. I walked in. There, in an armchair beside the fireplace, wrapped in a shawl, I saw her. 'Mammy,' I whispered, as I moved towards her and folded myself in her embrace.

I was home.

16.

HOME
APRIL 1943–FEBRUARY 1968

The following morning, all the family walked up the hill to our local church to attend mass and pray for my father. Afterwards, with my arm around my weeping mother, I walked with her among the granite headstones of the cemetery until we came to Daddy's grave. Despite all the carnage and loss of life that I had witnessed over the previous years, the sense of grief I felt in my heart was overpowering. The poor man had worked hard all his life to care for his family. He also had seen the horror and depravity that comes with war. It saddened me enormously that I never said goodbye, and that he never got to know I had survived. I found it extremely hard to come to terms with the idea that he wouldn't be around anymore.

Over the next few days, neighbours and friends called by to welcome me home. Some asked me to tell them where I had been and what the fighting was like. I always politely shied away from discussing it and tried to move the conversation along. It was only late at night, while sitting around the fire with my brothers and sisters, that I would give any indication of what I had been through. Nonetheless, the information I gave was scant because I found it too painful to relive some of the horrors that still haunted me.

'It was very tough at times. The fighting in France was horrific and our capture was terrifying, with us not knowing what they were going to do with us, or to us, at any moment. And then, the cold and the hunger; the bitter freezing and the pangs of starvation. I tell you, the dream of being here at home again kept me going.'

They all nodded and expressions of abhorrence of war were uttered. My younger sister Nora put her hand on my shoulder and told me that they knew I had been captured as a letter had arrived some years before telling them so.

'Yes, a lady called Doreen wrote from England. Imagine, all that was on the envelope was "Mr and Mrs McGrath, parents of Soldier Tommy, Portlaw". The lady said that she had heard that fella, Lord Haw Haw, on the radio and he had mentioned you being in a prisoner-of-war camp in Poland.'

'That's unbelievable.' I sighed. 'We were told that he was spreading propaganda alright and that the Jerries were giving him information, but I would never have thought he would have got my name. What did Mammy say?'

'It was a godsend for her. She broke down in tears when she read it. At least then we knew you hadn't been killed and it gave us all hope. It's a miracle, Tommy,' Nora said as she wrapped her arms around me in a warm embrace. How I had longed for this moment.

'To think that Haw Haw had helped me, and what a kind and thoughtful thing for that lady to do. Otherwise, you would have all thought I was a goner, just like Mary had concluded,' I said, lowering my eyes.

———

The following days were spent with me continuing my recovery. I would go for walks in the extensive woodlands of Curraghmore, meet old friends, or have fun with the local children, who were fascinated by my wristwatch, as they had never seen one before. I very much enjoyed holding them in awe in the evenings when I would point out an imaginary voyage through the constellations that I had learned from old Hamish in the camp. But underneath the euphoria I felt from being back home, there was always the deep sadness of having lost Mary. It caused a constant unease within me.

After two weeks, I was due to report back to Aldershot, from where I was to be redeployed to battle. I was torn inside. One part of me felt I had a duty to return to those friends I had left behind in the Stalag, but I also felt that, after what I had been through, I had done enough. Britain had conscripted me and forced me to war merely because I was working over there at the time. After all, I was now in Ireland, my country, which was neutral.

For days, I agonised over what to do. Although everyone had welcomed me with open arms, there was a constant niggling worry that many would have deeply disapproved of my serving in the British Army. Even though I had had no choice in the matter, I was troubled that they would not understand. Eventually, talking it through with my family, I made the decision to stay. The decision was heavily influenced by my mother, whose own two brothers were killed in battle the day after their return to France from leave during the First World War.

At the time, there was an understanding among the aristocracy that soldiers returning from war would be looked after and provided with employment. As a result, about a month after my return a representative of Curraghmore Estate called to the family home in Coolfin and offered me a job in the forestry division on the estate. He said that they knew I was a hard worker and that it was an opportunity to one day step into my father's shoes since he had run that section for years before he died.

I thanked him but said I would have to decline. I told him that I wanted to work somewhere quiet in the village. The reality was that I knew that working with a large group would make me uncomfortable, with persistent quizzing and enquiries about my experiences in the war and as a POW.

Two days later, the same man called again to the door. He asked if I would like to work for the local doctor and his wife, looking after their extensive gardens. I jumped at the offer and asked when I could start.

Dr Walker and his wife lived in a house called Springfield on the outskirts of the village. They were kind people who treated me very well. I tended to the gardens and on occasion I was asked to drive Mrs Walker into Waterford in their Austin motor car. They had been delighted to learn that I could drive because there were very few cars around and even fewer people who could drive them.

During my time with the Walkers, I had to bring the car to Wades' garage on the quays in Waterford for regular services or to have something or other fixed. During these visits, I got chatting with the mechanics and the manager. They clearly saw that I knew my way around under the bonnet of a car from my earlier training in Surrey. As a result, they very quickly offered me a job there, and I was delighted to accept.

Although, after two years working for them, I was sad to leave the Walkers and my family in Portlaw, I felt I needed to be independent again. I moved into digs in 40 Green Street, where I was looked after by the kind landlady, Cissy Latchford, who cooked my meals each day. It was ironic that in the adjoining street there was an Irish Army barracks from which I could hear the reveille each morning calling the soldiers to wake up.

I stayed working in Wades' for five years and got to know a lot of people and made many new friends. Over that time, there was a significant increase in the number of cars on the roads and business in the garage was booming. Other businesses were also beginning to pick up after the Emergency, as the period of the war was known as in Ireland. I saw an advertisement for a driver for an ice-cream company called Merville, delivering ice cream throughout the city. I applied and, I believe because of my driving experience, I got the job. I was delighted – not only did it mean more money, but at last I could work on my own.

Each day I would start my deliveries early in the morning and finish by six in the evening. I had to call to every news-agent, sweetshop, restaurant, hotel and cinema in the city. I quickly got the hang of it and really enjoyed both the work and the freedom that went with it.

The company let me have the use of the van at the week-ends so I could go to Portlaw to see the family. My nephews and nieces were always thrilled to see me because they knew I would take them for a spin in the van. Other times, I would go out for an evening with a friend or two to have a few drinks or go to see a film.

Sometimes at night, I would lie awake and think back about my time in the war. The memories tortured me. I also wondered how Mary was and if she was happy in her new life. I wished her well and I fully understood how she had believed I had been killed in action, not having heard from me, or about me, for nearly three years. No, life on my own was what I had now. I had to accept it and get on with it.

————

One day in 1950, I was doing my rounds and I called with the delivery to the Lido Café in Barronstrand Street in

Waterford city centre. As I was packing the freezer, I saw a lady walk into the shop, which was at the front of the restaurant. She stopped momentarily to check papers lying on a table. The girl behind the sweet counter saw me looking at the elegant woman and said, 'Have you met Miss Vaughan?' With that, Miss Vaughan turned around and our eyes met. We approached each other and shook hands. I told her my name and we exchanged a few pleasantries. She told me she was the owner and thanked me for the consistently prompt deliveries. I assured her that I would continue to do so.

From then on, each time I called to the Lido, as I parked my van outside I would cross my fingers that Miss Vaughan would be there when I went into the shop. To my amazement and delight, each time she was there, waiting to greet me. On each visit, we talked more and more. She asked me to call her Lil.

She had the warmest smile and a beautiful head of jet-black hair. To complement her looks, she was always dressed in great style, not at all flamboyant, but very tasteful. One day, I asked her if I could speak with her outside the café. There, I asked her if she would like to go out for a meal some evening. To my delight, she agreed.

As it happened, we went out for many meals and got to know each other. On one occasion, I suggested we should go for dinner to the Majestic Hotel in Tramore, which had a reputation for having good food and entertainment. As we entered the restaurant of the hotel, we were shown to a quiet table with a view overlooking the beach and sea. There was a piano tinkling faintly in the background.

Lil told me that she had grown up on a farm in north County Cork and that when she was younger she was called Lily, but since moving to Waterford she had changed it to Lil. I said I thought both names were beautiful. She said that as a child she had rheumatic fever and that the legacy of this caused a shortness of breath when under any physical strain.

'So, don't you have any expectations of having me running up and down that beach out there!' she joked, and then smiled. 'And as we are talking about names, Tommy, I am going to call you Tom from now on, if that's alright. It suits you better.'

'Whatever the lady wants,' I said, raising my glass. 'To Lil and Tom!'

I told her I was from Portlaw and I gave her a brief history of all my jobs over the years; from my working in the saw mills as a young man, my time with the Walkers, those years at Wades' garage, and then my current delivery position with Merville Ice Cream. At the time, I could not bring myself to mention my wartime experiences, nor could I summon the ability to even begin explaining that I was married.

Later, we did not go running on the beach, but while walking along it I felt very lucky to be with this lady whom I found to be so special. We strolled, each in our own thoughts.

Then I took her hand and stopped her. I turned and looked into her eyes.

'Lil, I have things I have to tell you. Things about me you need to know. I have very strong feelings for you, and I hope to God that what I am going to tell you won't affect how you feel about me.'

I told her everything: my marriage to Mary, my conscription into the British Army, my capture and the horrors of the Stalag. I told her I had seen things that no man should have to see and that could never be discussed with those who were not there. She stared at me with an intense yet compassionate gaze when I went on to relate the account of my escape. She hung on every word and exuded a warmth I had yearned for so deeply.

'So, Lil, I can never marry, as there is no divorce in Ireland. I can never return to Britain because I refused to go back to the army that had conscripted me, and I can never tell anyone about my past in the British Army for there are many who would say I am a traitor. I have told very few people about all this, only some of my family and, now, you.'

For a moment we just stood and looked into each other's eyes. Then I saw her lip curl and her eyes well up. She put her arms around me and began to sob, uncontrollably. Through gasping breath, she made sounds which, at first, I could not make out.

'I also have a secret, Tom, and I do hope you won't think

less of me when I tell you.'

Through the sobs, she went on to tell me how, as a young girl, she had had a relationship with a local boy and … and …

She began to tremble and collapsed into my arms. Her cries were inconsolable.

'I'm sorry, I can't, I can't go on. The pain eats into my heart,' she gasped.

I held her in my arms as she buried her head deep into my chest.

'It's alright, Lil, it's alright. There, there, easy, easy.'

She slowly raised her head and looked at me with eyes filled with sorrow; she sighed. 'I'm sorry, Tom, not now, not yet. One day, I will be able to tell you, I promise.'

Her sobbing subsided and we continued our stroll, only now my arm was around her and her head was resting on my shoulder. Shortly after, we had our first kiss, we said we loved each other, and we promised to support each other and find a way.

As the months went by, our relationship grew stronger and stronger. After work, I would go to the Lido and help with various tasks. Sometime after that, I left my job with Merville and, with Lil's sartorial advice, I bought a decent jacket, trousers, shirt and tie, and started working at the front of house in the restaurant. At the same time, we agreed that we would buy a car and I would offer my services as a hackney, which came in very useful for some of the Lido's customers.

Towards the end of 1951, Lil told me she was pregnant. We were both in shock. She was emotionally stunned, and I was ecstatic. Never in my wildest dreams did I think I was going to be a father. We were 'living in sin', Lil with a married man and now having a child out of wedlock. Despite these stigmas, we vowed that we would work out how to keep the baby and we both thanked God for giving us this blessing at this stage of our lives. Once again, we promised each other that we would find a way through.

As Lil was quite heavy-set, it was not difficult for her to conceal her condition for most of the pregnancy. For a few weeks before the baby was due, we moved to Cork, where we stayed in a hotel until the time came for Lil to be taken into the Glenvera private nursing home.

On 29 July 1952, my little boy, Thomas Joseph, arrived into the world.

———

Since we were not married, society would not allow for us to bring the baby back to live with us. Instead, I asked my sister Nora to mind him until I arranged for my youngest brother and his wife to look after the child for a time, until we could decide what to do. They were raising a young family in Kilkenny and a new baby would blend in easier, with no one any the wiser.

For nearly three years we visited our little son every weekend and doted on him every time we went. It broke our hearts to leave him each time we had to return home. A close bond had been formed with the little baby and, as we waved to say goodbye, his tears left us deeply distraught. After this time, we decided that we would take him home on the pretence that he was our nephew. He would call us Uncle Tom and Aunty Lil, and he was our Toddy. Our darling boy.

The unexpected joy of becoming a father had a profound effect on me. My life had gone from one of terror, starvation and despondency to one of love, care and responsibility. I discovered new emotions in myself, a sense of fulfilment. The joy of telling little Toddy bedtime stories about the little boy in a boat out at sea, caught in a storm, gave me huge satisfaction.

Shortly after we brought him home, I took Toddy to Portlaw to meet my mother and some of his uncles and aunts. Nanny McGrath, as she was known by all, was so very sweet with Toddy. She cuddled him up beside her on the couch by the fire and I had great difficulty getting her to let him go when it came to the time to go home. I could tell that she was very happy for me.

Each year, the three of us went on a short holiday to either Killarney, Ballybunion or a similar resort. Once, we considered going abroad to somewhere in the UK, but I was not prepared to risk the possibility that the British authorities had me on some list or other as a wanted man. Eventually, though, I decided I had to know. I wrote to the British Army and told them who I was and asked them where I stood in the eyes of the authorities. To my great relief, I got a reply to say that I had been granted a pardon under a government amnesty and that I was free to travel as I pleased. A short time after receiving the news, Lil and I went to the island of Jersey for a week's rest.

In the early 1960s, we made the decision to extend the restaurant and close the sweet shop. This was because of high demand, people were eating out more, and although the shop was making money, particularly from the patrons of the adjoining Savoy Cinema, nevertheless we saw ourselves as the leading place to eat out in town. We now had two large dining rooms, one upstairs and one downstairs.

It proved to be the right decision, because by the mid-1960s we had saved enough money to buy our dream investment. We had seen a large guesthouse next door to the Majestic Hotel in Tramore that was for sale, Rushmere House. We put in a bid, and we were successful. Apart from being a good investment, it was an opportunity for Lil to spend some time in the fresh air and to take time out from the responsibilities of running a busy restaurant.

In 1965, when Toddy was thirteen, we decided to send him to Rockwell College in Tipperary. We wanted him to have a good education and felt that boarding school was a better environment for him rather than living above the restaurant as he had done thus far. Toddy settled into his new life quickly and Lil and I visited one Sunday every month, the maximum number of visits permitted by the school, to take him out for a meal in Cahir or Cashel. You could see how much he enjoyed these treats because the boys were not allowed outside of the grounds except for going home on holidays.

———

In 1966, Lil's health deteriorated dramatically. We had befriended a Franciscan priest, Fr Aloysius, who visited Lil on a daily basis and gave her great comfort. In November, the doctor told me she had only days to live. I was distraught at the idea of breaking this terrible news to Toddy. He adored his mother and would be lost without her.

I asked a friend to go to Rockwell to bring him home. When he arrived, I could see how upset he was to see the semi-comatose state of Aunt Lil, his mother, lying helplessly in bed. He took her hand and hugged her. Before the next morning came, she had left us. It was 19 November 1966.

A few days after the funeral, I brought Toddy back to school. I thought he was better off being with his friends and getting distracted. Over the next eighteen months I visited him regularly and looked forward to when he would come home on holidays.

I now lived alone in the Lido, surrounded by memories of Lil. My life had become joyous with her, and it seemed cruel that she was taken from me so early. In truth, I took Lil's death very badly. I found myself brooding and down at heart. I confided in Fr Aloysius that I was concerned for my own health and worried what would happen to Toddy were I to die. I knew what being a survivor entailed and I wanted to spare my son that experience.

———

On Friday, 16 February 1968, I drove to Rockwell to bring Toddy home for the weekend, to give him a break. I did not get to see much of him as he was off with his friends most of the time, but the time together was precious. I loved hearing his stories of his activities in school and his enthusiasm as he explained the rules of rugby to me. He was getting to the age when we could have a serious conversation and I knew that the time would shortly come when I would have to tell him all that had been left unspoken.

On Sunday, I drove him back to school. When he got out of the car, and as I was about to drive away, our eyes met for a moment. I did not speak aloud the words that rose in my mind: *Go on, my boy, go on and make your life and be happy. Don't forget us. We loved you.*

Tom's prisoner of war card.

PART TWO

MY STORY

THIS IS MY STORY OF SEARCHING FOR MY PARENTS AND
DISCOVERING ALL THAT WAS LEFT UNSPOKEN

17.
WHAT I REMEMBER
1970s

My name is Tom. At least it is now. I changed it when I went to boarding school. As a child I was called Toddy, which to me sounded like a baby's name and not suitable for a grown up. But it was my parents' pet name for me, their only child. After all, if I was going to boarding school, I was all grown up.

I was born in Cork City on 29 July 1952. My father was Tom McGrath from Portlaw, County Waterford. My mother was Elizabeth Vaughan from Lismire, near Kanturk in north County Cork. I grew up in Waterford City, where my parents owned and ran the Lido Café. It was a thriving business and *the* place for people to go for a meal or just to sit with a cup of coffee. Any celebrity who came to perform in the city was sure to dine there. I remember many of the well-known showbands and international stars of the time, such as Roy Orbison, paying a visit before or after their show.

My earliest memories are of my mother laughing and chasing me around the kitchen in a playful way with a wooden spoon, of me rushing to jump out of her way into my father's arms. The thing is that while they were biologically my father and mother, and I loved them as such, when I was very small I only knew them as Uncle Tom and Aunty Lil. In fact, I was unable to say 'Lil', so I ended up calling her 'Aunty Nin'.

It may now sound hard to believe, but it never occurred to me to question whether or not they were my parents. They transformed from 'Uncle Tom' and 'Aunty Nin' to 'Tom' and 'Nin' as I got older. I think it is important to add that as a very small boy I grew up in a world of adults, so it was quite normal for me to call everyone by their first name. I was surrounded by a restaurant environment, with kitchen staff and dining-room staff rushing around tending to their duties. It was a very happy atmosphere, and they always found time to either play with me or say some kind words. Even though I never directly referred to my mother or father as my parents, they were who they were, and I accepted them wholeheartedly. That was my world, and I had no reason to ever consider questioning it. They were the personification of love and adoration.

My parents in their prime.

Because there was no divorce in Ireland at that time, my father was unable to enter into a new marriage with my mother since he still had a wife from before the war, despite that relationship having broken down.

From discussions that I have had with my new-found cousins, I have established that, immediately after I was born, I was first given to a sister of my father, who cared for me for some six months, after which I was then taken in by one of my father's brothers and his family. They lived in Kilkenny, which is less than an hour's drive from Waterford. I was told that my parents visited me every weekend and just before I was three years old, they took me to live with them in Waterford.

Being prominent businesspeople and highly respected, they could not openly say that I was their son, although I'm sure that it was suspected by all. They were extremely brave to hold on to me, because back then the most common fate that a child out of wedlock would have encountered was adoption. But they were not having any of that.

I have fond memories of both my parents, but because my mother died before my father, I remember more about him. Each morning he would bring me an egg flip, which is whipped eggs in hot milk, to wake me up.

My father would take me to dig up cockles by the sea, to pick mushrooms at dawn in the mist, and to make a valiant attempt at fly fishing, which I recall was not too successful because we lost the fishing rod when it fell over a waterfall!

I remember strolling on the long strand in Tramore beside him when I was very small. Suddenly, he would shout out in pretend surprise, 'There, over there!' and I would excitedly run to where he was pointing and discover a sixpence buried in the sand. Little did I know that while we were walking, he would throw the coins while I was distracted.

Finding coins in the sand.

One day, when I was a little older, we were sitting in the car waiting for a shower of rain to pass when I was talking about something or other and, for some reason, I used the word 'bloody'. Uncle Tom became furious with me and told me never, ever to use such language again. This is something that I find extraordinary, knowing what I now know about his time in the army.

He loved cars and enjoyed teaching me how to drive. At first, when I was really small, he would put me on his lap and let me steer the car while it was moving. When I was old enough to reach the pedals, he would let me drive short distances on back roads. I should point out that in those days there was very little traffic on the road, and I know that he was in control at all times!

At Saint Declan's, aged around 10.

For my first few years at primary school, he drove me there. And after school was over for the day, he would be at the steps in Saint Declan's, standing beside his striking two-tone maroon and cream Ford Zodiac, upright and dressed immaculately, in a poised, elegant stance. They were very happy days for me.

Recently, I met a few old friends who reminded me of a time when we were camping with the scouts in Stradbally, County Waterford. Over two hundred of us were sitting around tables at dusk, eating, when an ice-cream van pulled up beside the field where we had pitched our tents. Uncle Tom had arrived with a huge ice-cream cake for my birthday and ice creams for all the scouts.

My father was a happy and jovial man. However, at times of sudden distraction he would freeze and go into defence mode. He was always cautious and 'en garde' in an unexpected confrontation.

I saw him cry on only two occasions. From the age of around five I suffered terribly with warts on my knees. We tried everything, from sulphur to holy water. I didn't know it, but a decision was made that they were to be burned off in hospital. I was about seven or eight. I remember being on my back in theatre when I saw a man dressed in a white gown approach me with something in his hand. As it got closer, I could see the blue flame coming out of the top. Uncle Tom was holding me, and I saw that tears were streaming down his face. Looking back, I'm sure that I had been given local anaesthetic because I don't remember any pain, but I do vividly remember the tears.

My father's 'en garde' expression on Dublin's O'Connell Street.

My mother was a cheerful, generous and unassuming woman. She was always well turned out and fashionable, in a modest way. There was a certain innocence in her demeanour, a shyness, perhaps an aura of reserve. It is sad that the image I have engrained in my memory is of her constantly being out of breath. She could not walk up five steps without stopping for a few moments to recover. This condition was a legacy of her having had rheumatic fever as a child, which, in turn, caused damage to the valves in her heart.

Despite her ill health, Lil built up a thriving business in the centre of Waterford. She was obviously a good business-woman and turned the Lido into a huge success after buying it in the late 1940s. I was aware that she had been given a sum of money by her father that she used for this purpose. She worked hard and expected her staff to do likewise, but she treated them all very fairly.

My memory of my parents from when I was very small is of two hardworking people, full of life, both with a pleasant demeanour. They had a few select friends with whom they socialised, and Tom had a number of favourite local hostel-ries that he would frequent to play skittles and billiards. They were extremely generous both to their staff and others. In recent years, I have learned that they funded the education of some of my mother's nephews and nieces.

Growing up in a busy restaurant, with bustling dining areas upstairs and downstairs, and with a kitchen swarming with staff, was not the ideal environment for a child. As a result, it was not uncommon for me to spend the day looking for ways to entertain myself. I would often end up going to both the matinee and later sittings on the same day at the local cinema, on my own, a number of times each week. It did give me a vast knowledge of movies and actors of the time, which would have been something rare for a child of that age. Mind you, it did help with my acting skills when playing Cowboys and Indians – but, looking back, I can see that it was not ideal for a small child to spend so many hours like this.

Other days I would spend my time hitting a tennis ball against a wall or playing games with my local friends Johnny, Paddy, Niall, Noel and others. There was scouts too, which I enjoyed, but apart from that, there were no structured activities in which I participated. My parents wanted to do everything they could for me to ensure that I received a good education. When I was thirteen, they sent me to a boarding school, Rockwell College in County Tipperary. It was the best decision they could have made. It was my first exposure to organised sport and discipline, and it helped to knock the corners off me.

While life in Rockwell wasn't exactly bootcamp, it was not easy. It toughened me up from all the pampering that I had been showered with until then. That would stand me in good stead when my life as I knew it was changed instantly and for ever.

———

One morning, when I was about fourteen, I was sitting in class when I was called out and told to go to the president's office. A friend of the family was waiting for me. He told me that Aunt Lil was very ill and that he had been sent to bring me home. When I got there, I found my mother lying in her bed asleep, surrounded by a number of people. They were praying and repeating the rosary over and over.

Early the next morning I was awoken by my father with a gentle nudge to my feet. 'She's gone,' he said. I was taken in to see her laid out in the bed. It was the first time I had ever seen a body in that way. It struck me how peaceful she looked.

I remember the large funeral and walking with my father behind the hearse. Later, in the cemetery, small groups huddled together, nodding their heads in deep discussion. My mother was only fifty-three years old.

It was November. There was a cold chill in the air. For a time after, each night I would tuck myself up under the blankets and cry myself to sleep. I suspect that Uncle Tom did the same, although I never saw him doing so. For my benefit, he always put on a brave face and tried to create a cheery atmosphere. Sometimes, when he dropped his guard, I could see the deep sadness in his eyes. We both felt a huge void in our lives now that she was no longer with us.

Over the next eighteen months, Uncle Tom would drive to Rockwell to bring me home for the occasional weekend. During the holidays, I had my friends, particularly Johnny, to hang around with. Like any young lads, we had great fun.

On those visits home, there was a profound sense of sadness in the air. No matter how hard Tom tried to make life appear as normal, you could almost touch the void. Like most things in my life at that age, I simply accepted the circumstances. I missed her terribly and wondered where she had gone. In many ways, I had been prepared for this day. Since I was very little, both Tom and Lil would often playfully tell me that one day they would be gone. Looking back now, I believe that this was some inner defence against their greatest fear, that they would not live long enough to see me grow up. He was in his sixties and Lil, though only fifty-three, had suffered constant debilitating health throughout her life. Maybe they thought that by saying it enough times, it would never happen.

———

Shortly before my father died, he brought me home for a weekend. On one of the evenings, I walked into the sitting room, which was above the restaurant, and found him with his hands to his face, crying uncontrollably. I asked him what was wrong. He just looked at me and repeated over and over that Lil was gone and that he didn't know if there was any afterlife. I felt so helpless and guilty that there was nothing I could do to help him. That was the second, and final, time that I saw my father cry.

The following evening, he drove me back to Rockwell. I can remember the exact spot where we said goodbye. As I turned to walk away, I was struck by the look of sadness on my father's face as he waved his final goodbye to me. It is something that is seared into my soul and a moment I will never forget.

The next day, I got another tap on the shoulder. 'You are wanted in the president's office.'

By the time I got home, my father had died of a heart attack. He was sixty-four. In my research for this book, I found out that he had coronary atherosclerosis. Perhaps he had had a premonition that his time was nearly up.

I was brought to Maypark Hospital mortuary to see his body. I stood in the cold room with him. I still can sense the silence.

Saint Patrick's Church in Waterford is a quaint little chapel in a narrow laneway off a busy street. It was built in the mid-eighteenth century and is reputed to be the oldest Catholic church in Ireland. I sat in a pew at the front, waiting for the mass to begin. The rumble from behind made me aware that the nave was thronged with people. As I gazed from statue to statue of saints and angels in the now-familiar surroundings, my eyes kept being drawn back towards that which lay directly before me. The man I had known all my life, who had cared for and nourished me, the only person in the whole world who had been left for me to love, now he too was gone.

I have no memory of the service, but I vividly remember walking on my own behind the hearse as it slowly wound its way through the city streets, lined with people paying their respects. He had walked beside me on the previous occasion.

Later, at the graveside, I again stood alone. The sight of the coffin being lowered into the ground, followed by the thud of sodden earth being shovelled on top, is imprinted on my soul. Those sights left a mark on me, and I feel strongly that no child should be exposed to such images, if possible. It is only in recent years that I can bring myself to talk about them.

During my research for this book, I discovered that my parents paid for the refurbishment of Saint Patrick's Church, the same place where I stood to say goodbye to them both.

————

When my father died, the Lido was sold. Apparently, I was too young to have been told the ins and outs of the transaction. I was never told anything about the sale or how the assets were distributed or where all our personal effects ended up. This was very frustrating for me as I grew older and it had a huge influence on my decision to leave Waterford.

I was unaware of the extent of the contact that Tom continued to have with his brothers and sisters. I do have a vague memory of him bringing me to Portlaw when I was a toddler and meeting with a little old lady in a shawl. I believe that that was my paternal grandmother. On one occasion I was sent to London to stay with one of his brothers for a few weeks, where I worked as a teaboy on a building site in Holborn. I must have been ten or so. This alone points at there being some level of communication between my father and his siblings, but my guess is that it was minimal. Otherwise, I would have known about them. Lil also had had very little contact with her family, apart from one brother and his family in County Cork, whom we would visit each year. This may have been because she had a child out of wedlock.

After my parents' deaths, I heard nothing more from any of these relatives. Shortly after my father died, a woman called Mary, who worked in the restaurant and who had been taken on to help Lil with her ill health, told me in a cold and clinical manner that Uncle Tom and Aunt Lil were in fact my parents. This was the first time those words had been uttered to me, but I did not bat an eyelid. Her words meant nothing to me. In my heart, I had known it all along.

I suppose there is never a good time for your parents to die, but when they did, they had already left me well equipped to deal with it. Although I had a legal guardian, a lawyer who dealt with my parents' estate and held the purse strings, there was no real parent figure for me to look to. Having said that, boarding school had an enormous effect on my character and, as a result, I was at that stage developing an armour plate of independence which, because of where I now found myself, would grow even stronger. I became hugely interested in sport, particularly running. I would run for miles and miles through the fields and streets at a time when very few did so.

———

It is the end of the summer holidays. I am eighteen years of age, sitting on a cold floor in the waiting room of the train station in Saint-Jean-de-Luz. My rucksack is beside me. It is late and I am tired. It would be another hour before the overnight train would depart for Paris. Three hours earlier I had hopped on a bus from Bilbao after kissing my girlfriend, Asun, goodbye. We were both so very sad. I had spent the summer in a little town on the sea just outside Bilbao, where Asun was from. I stayed in the local campsite, and in the mornings I taught English to Spanish kids at a local school. We had the most wonderful, magical time in the world.

I met Asun on 12 July 1969 at a dance in the Haven Hotel in Dunmore East, County Waterford, while on holidays from Rockwell. We were both sixteen. She was a Spanish student who was spending the summer in Ireland to learn English. After the dance, I floated home singing her name and dreaming of 'Azul Martini'. It was only when we met again that I discovered her name was actually Asun Marti.

She was the girl who would change my life for ever.

With my future wife, Asun.

The following Saturday she couldn't meet me, so, instead, I stayed up all night to witness Neil Armstrong and Buzz Aldrin walk on the moon. I watched it on a small black-and-white TV, but even so, the hazy, grainy images left a huge impression on me. I watched it on my own, as I did most things. I had no brothers or sisters, or any cousins that I was aware of, and my parents were dead.

The Saturday after the moon landing, Asun and I met again at the dance. From that day on, we were inseparable for the rest of that summer. We had a special connection and each passing day we drew closer and closer. When she left to return home to Spain, the pain was unbearable, but we swore that we would stay in touch. And that we surely did. For the next ten months we would write to each other every day, and each day when her letter would arrive, my heart would have a little flutter of excitement.

The following summer, I went to Bilbao for a two-week holiday and stayed in the Hostal Amaya in Gorliz, just outside Bilbao. I was thrilled to discover that the flame in our young hearts burned as strong as ever – though, of course, I had never doubted it for a minute.

For the next seven years I travelled each summer, and then also every Christmas, to be with Asun. I taught English in schools and in private houses and I came to know and understand the culture of this wonderful new place in my life. For a young lad coming from rural Ireland in those days, it was the equivalent of being transported into the depths of South America or the Far East. It was an adventure, and it was magical.

Getting to Bilbao in those years was a challenge in itself. I would leave Dún Laoghaire at 5.30 p.m. on the ferry and get into Holyhead at close to midnight. From there I would take the overnight train to London's Euston Station and then a coach to Dover and travel across the English Channel by ferry or hovercraft.

There were no motorways, so the coach to Paris from Calais would take for ever but would arrive in time for me to catch the overnight train from Gare d'Austerlitz, which got into Saint-Jean-de-Luz early the next morning. From there I would cross the border into Irun, and there I would catch an Electrotren to San Sebastián. Finally, I would board the wooden train to take me me to Bilbao.

Over the years I did a number of variations of the journey. I got to know London and Paris quite well. When the ferry arrived in Calais, I would spend time walking around the military cemeteries, gripped by the rows and rows of unmarked white crosses. It made me wonder what terrible things must have happened in those very fields not so long before in the battles of World War II.

Asun's family welcomed me with open arms. They were conservative and quite religious. They treated me very well and did so despite me not having any tangible history or pedigree to show for myself. As the years went by, I became part of the family, and both her parents helped guide me on a professional course.

I was lucky to have met Asun when we were still very young. Since my parents were no longer alive for my final years at school and I had no knowledge of any other family at that time, on my breaks from boarding school I would either visit Asun in Spain or, for shorter school breaks I would go to Rushmere, the guesthouse my parents had owned in Tramore. Thinking back now, I remember I would always eat alone but, curiously, I never felt sad or lonely. Writing daily to Spain, or California, where Asun spent a scholarship year, gave me all the strength and drive I needed.

————

When I was nineteen, I moved to Dublin for university and did a degree in psychology and philosophy. I made new friends but was not much of a party-goer. I would still spend my nights writing letters to my 'Azul Martini'.

In my first year at college, I learned from a French student that the Federation of Railways in Europe was going to initiate a new student rail ticket called Interrail. I went down to the CIE office in Abbey Street a few times to enquire about this, but no one had heard of it. However, they very kindly said they would investigate it and, sure enough, a month or so later I was the happy owner of a brand new Interrail ticket, perhaps even the first in Ireland.

For the following two summers, prior to travelling to Spain, I went off to explore many other countries, broadening my horizons and coming across some interesting people and tricky situations. But through it all, my heart stayed loyal to Asun. I knew she was the person I wanted to build my life with.

Asun and I married on 11 September 1976 in a small church in the tiny mountain village of Garay outside Bilbao. She had finished her university studies and had obtained her degree in biochemistry. Back in Ireland, we moved into a small one-bedroom apartment in Rathmines. Asun began her PhD in University College Dublin while I studied to become a solicitor after completing my BA. We later moved to Rathfarnham, at the foot of the Dublin mountains, and it was there that we raised our two wonderful children, Eric and Cristina.

From an early age, I had always had a niggling yearning to find out more about my background, about my family history, about me. When we had children, the experience of being a father made me think more about my own early life and about my parents. I wanted to know more about their lives, to understand who they were and to find out about their respective family backgrounds. I feel this compulsion must have radiated from me to my children because, from a very young age, they had been longing to find something or someone to guide them to their Irish heritage. It became a journey that we embarked on together, as a family.

18.
DISCOVERING UNCLE TOM, MY FATHER

O ver the years I often thought about how I could find any relatives. Seven years ago, in 2015, I decided to commission a genealogical report from a respected genealogist, Paul Gorry. He had been recommended to me by a friend, Fergus Gillespie, the retired Chief Herald of Ireland, with whom I had been speaking about my aspiration to explore my family history. After a lot of research, Paul provided me with a detailed report on my McGrath and Vaughan family backgrounds, which I gave to Eric and Cristina as a Christmas present that year.

From the report, I was able to glean that my father was born into humble surroundings on 17 January 1904 and that he had ten siblings. On the other hand, the report showed that my mother came from a family of wealthy landowners in north County Cork. She was born on 25 April 1913 and was one of seven siblings.

I was astounded to discover from the report that my father, when very young, had married a local woman named Mary Fowler in Portlaw. When Cristina read the report, she did some research online and managed to locate a niece of Mary Fowler, also called Mary Fowler, living in Portlaw. She located her phone number and I called Mary and arranged to travel to Portlaw to meet her with Cristina.

We had a very pleasant lunch with Mary, who turned out to be a lovely, warm lady who said that she remembered my father from her days working in a shop next door to the Lido,

The square in Portlaw around the time my father was born.
(Courtesy Waterford Museum)

RTV Rentals, when she was very young. She knew about the breakdown of the marriage but said that whenever her aunt came over to visit her family in Portlaw from the UK, my father would travel to Portlaw to meet her, because they had remained on amicable terms. Knowing my father, I am sure that he understood how Mary could have assumed that he was never coming back from the war and entered another relationship in such a belief. Mary told me that her aunt did eventually remarry, once she could legally do so after my father died.

Before we left, Mary showed us a magnificent, engraved tea set she said had been given to my father and her aunt as a wedding present, and it had remained in her family ever since. She then said that she wanted me to have it because she felt that it was destiny that had made her keep it all these years. I thanked her profusely and said that I was very touched by her kindness.

My daughter, Cristina, and me meeting Mary Fowler.

When the children were younger, I would sometimes bring them down to Portlaw and they would innocently stop people and ask if they knew of any McGraths. We never got lucky. That is, until November 2016.

Cristina had given me a birthday present of three tickets to the Ireland versus Australia autumn season rugby match. I asked her then fiancé, now husband, Ken, and his dad, John, to come with me to the game. Over lunch before the match, we had the usual chit-chat about this and that. When I told John that I had grown up in the centre of Waterford, he asked if I knew a man called Johnny Aylward, an acquaintance of his. I said I remembered him as a young man, although he was probably in fact a teenager when I was a small boy. His family had a well-known bar across from the Lido, and I said to pass on my regards. A few days later, John called me and told me that Johnny did remember me and that he had lots of stories about the Lido and that he would love to meet me. Some weeks later, I travelled to Waterford, had lunch with Johnny, and we walked around the city reminiscing. He told me a number of stories about my father, my mother and the Lido. We agreed we would keep in touch. A few days later he sent me an email and gave me the name and phone number of somebody whom he said I might like to contact. The name was Billy McGrath.

I called the number and spoke with Billy and discovered that he was my first cousin, a son of my father's brother Willie. Billy is one of nine children of Willie and his wife Minnie, both deceased. I arranged to meet with Billy and his brothers and sisters some months later. Having never known of my family, this was exciting new ground for me.

On 16 March 2017, I drove from Dublin to Waterford for the meeting. During the journey, I kept thinking over and over about how fortuitous an occasion this was going to be. After so many years of searching, the moment had arrived when I would meet not the one or two cousins that I had thought I might find, but tonnes of them! It was an engaging yet poignant thought. I am not religious, but I did wonder whether strings were being pulled up there in the great firmament and if Tom was looking down with a contented smile.

I met seven of my cousins in the Tower Hotel in Waterford. Of course, I had spoken by phone with most, if not all, of them in the previous few months and I knew in my heart that it was going to be a very special event. Indeed, it turned out to be a very emotional moment from the first time that Billy and I met in the car park when he kindly came out to assist me. Our eyes met and something happened. It was immediately as though we had known each other all our lives. There was a deep attachment, and our eyes welled up as we embraced. It was extraordinary. He brought me into the hotel to meet the others and I spent nearly four hours talking with them. A strong sense of affection enveloped our little group. They told me many stories about my father, who some of them had known, being older than me. While I had not known of their existence, they did know of me but did not know where in the world I was or where to find me.

Six weeks later, Asun and I again went down to Waterford to have lunch with my new-found cousins. All nine were now present with their spouses. Before the meal I announced that I wanted to share a few words. I said that for over forty years I had attended many of Asun's family reunions and meals where I was the odd one out. However, on this occasion, that honour was Asun's. There had been an imbalance up to then since Asun comes from such a large family and they have, accordingly, many Spanish relatives. I thanked them for helping my children find their Irish heritage.

I got great satisfaction from listening to my new-found cousins tell me things about my father that I never knew. The older ones remembered him for his kindness in helping their family, particularly when they had to move from Portlaw to Waterford City after their father, Willie, became unemployed following the closure of the tannery in Portlaw. It seems that on each Christmas Eve my father would arrive to their house with a bagful of toys – more than likely leftovers from his spoilt son. As they grew up, they kept in touch with him now and then.

My eldest cousin, Brendan, could recall swarms of children gathering at the bridge in Portlaw, listening to Tom's stories. At night he would point out the various stars and constellations in the sky. Brendan told me that he was always joking and pulling harmless pranks with the kids. In fact, he said he had a vivid memory of walking home one night when

Tom frightened the living daylights out of him by making spooky noises from behind a bridge under cover of darkness.

He remembered that my father was always impeccably turned out, and that he worked as a gardener for Mrs Walker, who lived in the town. Sometime after he arrived back in Portlaw, he moved to Waterford to work in Wades' garage as a mechanic and he later got a job as a driver for Merville Ice Cream, delivering to local shops and restaurants.

In fact, an amazing coincidence occurred shortly after meeting my cousins. I paid a visit to Portlaw with my cousins Brendan and Dick. Brendan directed me to drive up a little hill at the edge of the town and asked me to stop outside a house with a large garden: Mrs Walker's house. At that very instant my son Eric called me on my mobile phone from Melbourne, where he was living at the time. As I peered into the garden, in my mind's eye I could see my father looking out at us, observing his son in a car with his nephews and with his grandson listening in on a phone from far away in Australia. It was a very emotional moment.

Brendan told me that he never forgot two things in particular about my dad. The first was that he was always turned out immaculately and his shoes would shine bright from polishing. The second thing that stuck in his mind was that whenever Tom heard anyone complaining about the cold weather, he would turn and say, 'Sure that's a summer's day in Poland.' As a child, Brendan had no idea where

Poland was, but he knew that it must have been a bitterly cold place.

It is quite possible that Tom met Lil while he was working for Merville. When I was born, as stated previously, I was given to a sister of Tom's, Nora, who looked after me. After six months I was then sent to live with a brother of Tom's and his family in Kilkenny. My cousins told me that Tom and Lil used to visit me every weekend, without fail. When I was three years old, they came to take me to live with them in Waterford.

It seems that because I had been born out of wedlock, which in those days was a colossal disgrace, a plan was initiated whereby I would be gradually introduced to the burghers of the city of Waterford. And so little Toddy was taken in by 'Uncle Tom' and 'Aunt Lil'.

———

Over the past three years, my family and I have become very close to my cousins. Shortly after our meeting, we were invited to the wedding celebrations of one of their children, Sonya, held at the Haven Hotel in Dunmore East – the very same place where I had met 'Azul Martini' all those years before.

A few weeks before that first meeting in March, I received a phone call from my new-found cousin Rita, who lives in

London. We spoke at length and, after some time, she told me that her mother, Minnie, had known my father very well. Her family was living with Tom's mother in Portlaw when he returned from the war. She remembered them all sitting around the open fire in the evenings, talking for ages. Rita herself was too young at the time to know, or even remember, what was being said. She went on to say that Minnie had been a member of a creative writers' club and that she had written an essay about my father entitled 'The Escape', which she vaguely remembered being about my father's escape from a prisoner-of-war camp. She did not have any details but said that she would try to find the essay and send it to me.

The mere fact that there was even a suggestion that Tom had been a prisoner of war ignited a fire in my belly to find out exactly what had happened to him. When I received the short essay, I was astounded at its content. Was this courageous man, this hero, really my dad? It turned out to be one of the defining moments of my life and set me on a course that has changed that life for ever.

I immediately wrote to the British Army Records Office and began a thread of correspondence with them. After some months, I received my father's army service file from them. Attached to the files was a rusty paper clip with Tom's photograph in uniform, taken on his conscription. The service file stated, among other things, that Thomas McGrath was enlisted on 12 October 1939. He was aged thirty-five and gave his profession as chauffeur. He was posted to Aldershot Training Centre. Armed with all this information, I was now determined to try and find supporting evidence that what Minnie had written was true. I phoned various authorities in Britain, and all said that it was highly unlikely that I would find the information I was searching for.

I decided to go to London to conduct research directly at the National Archives in Kew. It is a fascinating place. You can see people from all walks of life, an eclectic mix, carrying out research into an endless treasure of history, from parchment to print. Mind you, it does take time. You must register, obtain a Reader's Card and view a training video on how to handle the precious and fragile documents, search for them, and if you are lucky to find what you are looking for … you wait.

After some hours of searching, I came across a reference to my father's serial number, T117287, and I filled in an application form for any documents that might have been held in their vaults. Once submitted, I was assigned a table with a locker with a clear glass window labelled with the same reference number as on the form. When an order has been retrieved from the archives, it is placed in the locker to await collection.

Having waited for over an hour and a half, out of the corner of my eye I sensed a shadow on the other side of my locker, so I looked up to see a staff member place a blue leather-bound tome in it. I slowly opened the door to pick it up and touched the frayed cover with my fingertips. I was overcome with trepidation, anticipation and anxiety as to what, if anything, I might find. On opening the book, I saw that it was marked 'top secret' and contained a number of typed reports of soldiers' experiences during World War II. There was no index, but it was not long before the name *Cpl McGrath, Thomas*, jumped up at me. I had found him!

The typed account was entitled 'Most Secret Account of Escape of Cpl. McGrath, Thomas'. This was a formal record of my father's escape story as recounted by him to MI5, MI6 and the American Army on his return to England.

As I began to read, I sensed that this was a very special moment that was meant to happen. He deserved for it to happen. It was destiny. I cast my eyes over the typed words, feeling astonishment, wondrous amazement and enormous pride. I also felt a pang of frustration at not having been aware of this incredible story, which should have had the recognition it deserved. I photographed the account and walked out of the building as if in a trance. Some hours later I called my family and told them what I had discovered.

The following day, before flying home, I paid a visit to the Imperial War Museum and researched what I could about the British Expeditionary Force and the 51st Highland Division, because the records indicated that this was the army regiment my father had been assigned to and which formed part of the army sent to France in 1939. In my research, I had learned that in mid-January 1940, the 51st Highland Division departed from Southampton and disembarked in the French port of Le Havre. Later that month, the division came under the command of the British Expeditionary Force. It seems that the weather conditions in France were atrocious, and it was apparently one of the worst winters on record. There are accounts of the ground freezing, only to turn to mud and slush when it thawed. It must have been so difficult for the poor men to dig trenches and carry out training in these conditions. From what I could gather, this was their only activity for months because of the French government's policy of relying on defence instead of pushing back the invaders. Of course, after this period, the regiment was thrust into the reality of bitter battle, leading to many soldiers' deaths.

All this information was fascinating. What anecdotes and adventures my father could have told me! The danger he had been exposed to and the unbearable fear he must have had to endure. I felt so proud and yet so very sad that the poor man had to carry all that inside him for the remainder of his life, without telling anybody.

Since finding out all these incredible facts about my father, never once did it cross my mind to feel in any way hurt or let down that he had never told me. I empathise with him wholeheartedly. My greatest sentiment is sadness for all that he went through and, if anything, I feel a tinge of shame that it never crossed my mind to ask him about his life. I do know for sure that had he lived just a short while longer, he would have told me everything, and that I would have been as proud as a peacock to learn the truth of his life before me.

———

Sometime after discovering my father's wartime experiences, I decided that it was appropriate to combine both my parents' deteriorating headstones into one new unit with updated text to include reference to their heroic lives:

> *Lil, most generous and caring,*
> *a determined businesswoman ahead of her time.*
> *Tom, so brave and modest of his war-time heroism,*
> *forever warm and loving.*
> *While both endured tremendous hardship,*
> *they remained unconditionally devoted to each other*
> *and to their loving son, Toddy.*

Shortly after the new headstone was put up, Asun and I drove to Tramore to view it. Standing there, I felt an enormous rush of pride. I was so grateful that I had been able to discover so much about their lives and to commemorate them in this way. I felt a deep sadness at their absence, but also a deep respect for how they had chosen to live their lives. For me, their son, it was inspiring and humbling.

19.

DISCOVERING AUNTY LIL, MY MOTHER

In August 2019, I was invited to give a talk about my father's escape. It was held in the Heritage Centre in Portlaw, and it was a very successful evening. There was a full house and I believe that those who attended found my description of my father's heroic achievements to be of great interest. A few weeks later, the curator of the centre wrote to me and said that he had been asked by someone for my contact details. I asked him to please pass them on.

Shortly afterwards, I received an email from a person called Denis Vaughan, who explained that he was a first cousin on my mother's side. I phoned him, and he told me that he had come across details of my father's wartime story some time before but did not know how to find me. He told me that he remembered my mother well and that he had been very fond of her. He had also met my father a number of times.

Denis went on to say that each year for the past ten years or so, he had been going on holidays with friends to Tramore. The first year there, he decided to look for my mother's grave as he had been at her funeral and knew that she was buried in Tramore. He found it and had continued to visit it each year since. However, on his most recent visit, he got a huge surprise when he saw that the headstone had been recently replaced. When he read on it the reference to my father's wartime experience, he researched it online and found the full story. As a result, when he came across the newspaper coverage of my talk in Portlaw, he set out to contact me.

A week after our very first call, Asun and I met up with Denis at the Imperial Hotel in Cork.

Meeting my cousin Denis for the first time.

Denis, who is older than I am, is the son of my mother's eldest brother, Jack Vaughan. I enjoyed listening to the many stories he recounted about my mother. Although he would have been quite young at the time, he remembered when she and my father came to visit the old family home in Lismire.

After a few hours of reminiscing, I told Denis that over many years I had come to the conclusion that Lil, my mother, had been ostracised by her family because she could never marry my father since he was already married. I said that I believed that she was a very strong woman to raise me, in the circumstances, because in those different days, adoption would have been the most probable outcome for me.

With that, I noticed a sudden change in Denis's eyes. I could nearly hear his thoughts churning around in his head.

'I have something on my mind, and I don't know how I should say it, or whether I should even say it,' said Denis.

'Well, the genie is out of the bottle now. You're going to have to say it,' I replied.

Denis paused, took a deep breath, and very slowly let out the staggering words, 'Your mother had a child when she was in her twenties. She and the child's father wanted to get married, but her father forbade it and made her give the baby up for adoption.'

Asun and I looked at each other in shock. What a bombshell! Once I had regained my composure, I went on to ask a few questions. Did Denis know whether the baby was a boy or a girl? It was a boy, said Denis. I then asked him who the father was. He gave me a name and told me that he went on to have another family but that he was long deceased. He also shared with me the name of another one of this man's sons, which I took a note of.

I thanked him for telling me and told him that he had done the right thing, as it was something that I was entitled to know. I was both elated and yet very sad to find out. All my life I had been an only child and now with this startling revelation, that was no longer the case. My world was changing rapidly.

Throughout this whole journey, from the very beginning,

new details constantly continued to emerge about my family. In fact, in most cases, the information comes to me while I am not even actively searching for it. Such are the curveballs of life.

Now it was clear that I had been right all along. My mother had been ostracised, not because of me, but because of my half-brother. Whoever he was and wherever he may be, if still alive, I said that I would do everything I could to find him. I owed it to him and to our mother to do so. Denis asked how I felt about what he had told me. I said that, with my background, nothing fazes or surprises me anymore.

Driving back to Dublin after meeting Denis, I couldn't get what he had told me out of my mind. I was so glad that he had reached out to me and felt a strong connection with him as someone I could trust. He exuded a warmth towards me and a sense of care and sympathy for my past. Similar to the earlier meeting with the McGrath cousins, there was an immediate bond between us.

Later that evening a strange emotion came over me. I felt as if I was living my life in a trance. What else was going to emerge from the past to test the bounds of plausibility? It was incredible, but at the same time, for me, it was very satisfying.

The next day I contacted the genealogist Paul Gorry, who had assisted me before, and told him the news. I gave him as much detail and information as I had. Paul said that it was not going to be easy to trace the record of the birth, but that he would start to work on it.

Over the next few weeks we exchanged emails and texts and spoke on the phone. Then one day, during the course of one of these calls, Paul asked me what my mother was known as. I told him that, although her first name was Elizabeth, I had known her to be called Lil.

'That's it, I've got her!' shouted Paul down the phone, 'Lily Vaughan gave birth to a baby boy called Patrick on 17 March 1939 in Bessborough Mother and Baby Home in Cork.'

I was delighted with the news and asked Paul did he know where we could find the records of the home. He said that he believed that they were probably destroyed, because the home had been under investigation in recent years for alleged atrocities committed there. He told me that he would get back to me.

Some days later, Paul informed me that the records were in existence, but were not available to the public. He gave me a phone number and a name, which I called. I was told that my application to find out where Patrick was would take six months. I gave the details, and the clock began ticking.

———

I learned from the genealogical report that Lil was born in 1913 and grew up on a farm in north County Cork. Her father had lived in the United States long before she was born and had accumulated significant wealth there – enough that years later he could afford to buy farms for a number of his sons. His daughters, Elizabeth and Noreen, on the other hand, were destined for a different future.

Lil's childhood was not easy. Growing up on a farm that was miles from anywhere meant that each day she had to walk for over an hour to school and back. Playing with friends was a luxury she seldom enjoyed. Her parents were religious and strict, particularly her father. After doing her homework, it was expected that she would help with whatever work was required in the house or in the farmyard.

When she finished her schooling, her parents sent her to work on her brother's farm in Churchtown, near Buttevant, County Cork. This continued into her mid-twenties when she then met a local boy, the son of a nearby farmer. They began seeing each other and, after some time, she discovered that she was pregnant. When she did, her whole world caved in. In Ireland during the 1930s – and indeed up to the late 1980s – having a child outside of wedlock was the greatest sin a girl could commit. It was seen as bringing shame not only to the poor girl, but to her entire family. Indeed, from contemporaneous records I discovered that, to compound matters, the father of the child was recorded as being a Protestant. This magnified the sin a thousandfold. However, during my research, I discovered that Patrick's father was in fact a Catholic. Apparently, many of the records for children born out of wedlock cannot be relied upon because it was common for people in fearful circumstances to provide false information to hide identities.

This must have been a very distressing time for Lil, or Lily as she was known then. At first, I'm sure, she would have been too afraid to tell anyone she was pregnant. No doubt she must have felt terribly alone and surely dreaded the day when her father would find out. Inevitably, he did. My understanding from conversations with family is that he forbade her from seeing the boy again and, with the aid of the local priest, he arranged for her to be taken to Bessborough Mother and Baby Home in Cork City. I had not heard of this institution until recently, but I have since discovered what a truly horrendous place it was. It was common for the nuns there to insult and deride the girls for casting shame on their families. It must have been extremely difficult for Lil.

Bessborough House is a three-storey Georgian mansion located in the Blackrock area of Cork. It is an impressive building surrounded by high walls and clusters of dense trees and shrubbery, which lends it an air of isolation. It was taken over by the nuns of the Sacred Hearts of Jesus and Mary in 1922 for use as a convent. Shortly afterwards, it became one of the first of the now infamous mother and baby homes in Ireland. These state-supported institutions received public funds and were subject to state inspection.

From extensive research, I have learned that all the girls who entered this institution had the same three things in

common: they were all unmarried, they were all pregnant and they were all made to shoulder a heavy burden of
tremendous shame. The nuns never missed an opportunity
to remind the girls of what terrible sinners they were.

On admission, each girl had to hand over all her belongings, including her purse and any jewellery. They were told
that they would have to change their names for the duration
of their time in the home and that at no point could they leave
the grounds. They were then given a starched uniform and
sandals and told to follow a nun to where they were shown
into a large dormitory, which contained around thirty beds.
The nun would point to the bed that each girl was to sleep in.

There were no showers. In the mornings, the girls washed
in handbasins which were outside the toilets. The food was
meagre and of poor quality, and barely sufficient to sustain
pregnant girls who were also assigned physically demanding
daily tasks such as scrubbing floors and laundry work. At
night, it was difficult to find sleep in a dormitory of sobbing,
lonely and frightened girls.

There were no calendars on the walls, but in each girl's
heart there was the gnawing awareness that each day that
passed brought closer the time when the baby that she had
carried and nourished for nine months would be born and,
almost certainly, taken away for ever.

Unlike most of the other girls, Lil entered Bessborough on
the day she went into labour to give birth to my half-brother,

Patrick, who was born on Saint Patrick's Day 1939. She was given the house name Mary Pat and her son was immediately taken away from her.

Cyril/Patrick's birth record.

From the records, I have established that my mother remained in Bessborough for a further thirty-six days. From research and taking into account her background, I would assume that she was not made to do very much work and, overall, her life there was not any way as harsh as it was for the others. It can also be assumed that this was a result of a generous contribution being paid to the institution by her father. There is reference in the records of women having to buy their freedom in order to be released from Bessborough.

I can only speculate as to why my mother stayed in Bessborough for so long after the birth. I wonder was it perhaps to allow things to settle back home, both in the house and in the townland? Maybe she also needed to recover physically and mentally too, having gone through such an ordeal. This would enable her to slip back seamlessly into the community.

I felt that not only did I owe it to our mother to do all in my power to close this circle that had begun when I discovered my father's story, but there was also a primal yearning driving me to find the brother I had never known. I took every step that I could think of to find Patrick. I commissioned a genealogical report, searched endless online databases and awaited a response from the relevant adoption agency to which I had applied for information. I even submitted a DNA sample to two global companies in the hope that some more clues might show up, but alas, nothing did.

Then one day I got a call from a lady, Ms J., of Tusla, the child and family protection agency, to say that she had been assigned the case and that she had carried out some research into the file. She asked if I could meet with her, and a week later, Eric and I drove down to Cork. We met Ms J., who explained that she had found my brother, and that she had just recently spoken with his daughter. Unfortunately, however, she informed me that he had passed away the previous January.

The words hit me like a thunderbolt. It was the last thing I was expecting. I know that sounds odd, but I was waiting for news that she was working on the case and that we should expect it would take time and so on. But the previous January. God no. I had missed him by a few miserable months.

We spent over two hours with Ms J. I told her the whole background of Lil and Tom and of finding cousins late in life. I became quite emotional when telling her that, after all that Lil had been through with Patrick, she was deprived by society from ever being able to call me her son and had to endure my calling her Aunt Lil.

Ms J. is one of the kindest and most professional people I have ever met. It was she who told me all the information I know about Lil's stay at Bessborough. She told me that Patrick had been reared in a happy foster home and when adoption was introduced in Ireland, he himself applied to be formally adopted by the family. His letter was on the file in Ms. J's possession. She suggested that he probably did this around the time he was getting married, in order to formalise his situation.

Thirteen years after Lil gave birth to Patrick, she would return to Cork City to give birth to another son – me – in Glenvera Nursing Home. A place geographically quite close to Bessborough but, on an emotional level, a million miles apart.

It took some time for the enormity of all these new revelations to sink in. It made me look back and think of my mother. Now I could understand, now I could see why she was always so reserved, almost fragile, but with a smile, a heart of gold, and a backbone of steel. It pains me enormously to think of how much she suffered in her short life with the tragedy of her child being taken from her. How I wished I could hold her in an embrace and tell her that it had all worked out well, that Patrick went on to have a happy and rewarding life and that she could be proud of the wonderful grandchildren she has from both her sons.

With Ms J. acting as intermediary, a time was arranged for Patrick's two daughters, Angela and Marie, to call me. They both lived in London. When they first heard the news of my existence, they were taken aback. Their father had told them, once they were adults, that he had been adopted, but he had strongly resisted their encouragement to seek any information about his parents. He always said that he did not want to know.

Patrick was taken away from Lil on the day he was born. A priest knocked on the door of a kind and benevolent family in Cork and said, 'I have another one for you.' The family took the infant into their foster care. And since there were already two other males named Patrick in the family, my brother was renamed Cyril. He grew up in Cork, in what appears to have been a very loving and happy environment. At seventeen, he followed his foster brother to England and began working at a car-manufacturing plant in Dagenham. He remained in that job for many years until he took redundancy and then worked in security in the parliament buildings in London. This was no mean feat for a lad from Cork in the 1970s, particularly in view of the ongoing IRA campaign at the time.

Denis had told me that the name of Patrick's father was well known in the locality where he and Lil lived at the time.

He had also said that this man had gone on to have a family in later life, some of whom still resided in the same area. Armed with this, albeit sketchy, information, I decided to visit the area to see if I could get any clues that would help me find out about my brother.

After an exhausting day of endless enquiries, I was eventually given the name and phone number of someone I was told could assist me. Later, I met with this person, who turned out to be a son of Patrick's father; in other words, a half-brother of Patrick, just like me.

I approached the subject with the delicacy and the respect that it deserved. When I told him what I had discovered, he was astounded. He had never heard anything about this before. We sat down for a coffee and had a lengthy conversation, after which we agreed we would both continue our respective enquiries and keep in touch. When we next spoke, some months later, he told me that from his own investigations, the story had been confirmed. Since then, we have remained in contact, and I keep him informed about our mutual new-found nieces, whom he is looking forward to meeting someday.

———

In February 2020, Asun and I flew over for the day to London to meet Angela and Marie and their respective families. We landed in horrendous weather at London City Airport. I knew immediately that the two smiling, elegant ladies in the arrivals area were my nieces. They took us to Marie's beautiful home where a fabulous lunch had been prepared by her husband, Dean. Glass of wine in hand, we pored over family albums of what had clearly been a very happy childhood for them.

Cyril/Patrick, the brother I never knew.

Cyril was an adoring family man, hardworking and with a contagious sense of fun. His wife, Rita, had predeceased him and, following that, his health and spirit deteriorated. Marie said that she thought that if I had found him while he was still alive, he might not have wanted to know me and that it would have been very painful for me. I said that I understood, but I would not have given up on reaching out to him.

Angela and Marie told us about the family, their family, who had taken in their father as a new-born and how he was brought up with tender loving care as one of their own. They reminisced about the many happy holidays they had enjoyed in their youth with them in Cork.

It was a very emotional and rewarding visit. At one point during the lunch, I looked up at Marie and whatever way the light caught her features, I saw my mother. Tears filled my eyes. Twenty-five per cent of my nieces' DNA was my mother's. I wanted to hug them.

My nieces and I now keep in regular contact. In fact, they created a WhatsApp group with Lil's photograph as the group image and named the group, 'Lil's Family'. We have developed a warm and loving relationship and I feel so fortunate that they have come into our family's life.

Asun and I meeting our nieces, Angela and Marie,
for the first time.

Lil could never have imagined that I would ever have discovered her deep secret about the child she had to give away as a young girl, not to mention that I would come to locate him some day. I am sure that it would be a huge relief to her to have the burden of carrying such a weight on her shoulders finally lifted. I know the immense satisfaction it would give her to know how much she will be so admired by families of both her sons.

Some months later, I asked Marie for the address of Cyril's adoptive family. I said I wanted to write to them to say who I was and to thank them sincerely on Lil's behalf for the love they had shown her son.

A short while after writing to them, I received a very warm reply from one of the family and we said that one day we would meet to say hello.

20.

HOW I FOUND MY PARENTS

The following sections are the results of years of research, interviews and travel to various locations. It was hard work, but I relished every moment of it.

There are many avenues I explored but, ultimately, I believe that my progress was thanks to two essential ingredients that must form the foundation of any such undertaking: an unwavering passion to find out the truth and a strong determination. Armed with these two traits, it is amazing to discover how doors can be opened, treasures revealed and hidden surprises brought to light. A sprinkling of luck doesn't go astray either. Of course, once you find out where to look, it is essential that the people you meet show a willing disposition to help. I am glad to say that I have been fortunate in this regard, and I am so very grateful to those whose paths I crossed who gave generously of their time and extended a humane kindness that I will never forget.

In my experience, I found that sourcing a genealogy report was a good place to start. It gave me a resource to draw from and added structure to what had been, up to then, a more haphazard approach. However, if that had not revealed anything, I know that I would have explored all options and knocked on other doors. That hunger and determination to find out my family's past would have driven me to look under every rock.

1. MY FATHER'S WAR MEDALS

Rumb. 36037

2517

FIFTH SUPPLEMENT
TO
The London Gazette

Of FRIDAY, the 28th of MAY, 1943

Published by Authority

Registered as a newspaper

War Office, 1st June, 1943.

The KING has been graciously pleased to approve the following award in recognition of gallant and distinguished services in the field:—

The Military Medal.

No. T/117287 Corporal Thomas McGrath, Royal Army Service Corps.

The London Gazette, *May 1943, announcing Tom's medal award.*

When I first received the service file from the British Army, my daughter, Cristina, searched the internet armed with her grandfather's army serial number to see what she could find. She came across a citation in *The London Gazette* of May 1943 announcing that King George VI had awarded my father the Military Medal.

I wrote to the Army Medals' Board of the British Army to enquire if my father had ever received his reward. After protracted correspondence, a year later I received notification to say that my father had not received the award and, since he did not return from leave, he had forfeited the right to it. I replied requesting for the decision to be appealed. Initially, I got nowhere, but when I put forward my argument based on the points outlined below, I heard back that my appeal had been formally lodged.

My points of appeal were:

- The Prime Minister, Winston Churchill, had granted an amnesty for such soldiers on Queen Elizabeth's coronation in 1953.
- I provided at least eight precedents from World War I where soldiers had had their medal awards reinstated under comparable circumstances.
- I explained that my father had been conscripted to fight for a country that was not even his. Nonetheless, he had obviously done so diligently for within a matter of months he had been promoted to corporal.
- He had engaged in fierce warfare in the Battle of France.
- He had been captured and subjected to horrendous treatment at the hands of the enemy.

Some six months later, I received word that a decision had been made and that I would be formally notified in due course. In December 2018, I received a most gracious letter from Lieutenant Colonel Kestrel Simson. We were over the moon. Not only was my dad being awarded one medal, he was now getting three!

Dear Mr McGrath,

Firstly, can I apologise for the length of time that it has taken to provide an answer to your original and seemingly simple question from July last year asking whether your father had ever collected his Military Medal. The straight-forward answer is that he was never presented with it.

Your father's story has generated a great deal of discussion. What is clear and factual is that your father joined the British Territorial Army in October 1939 at the outbreak of the 2nd World War initially serving with the 51st Highland Division. He and the Division were sent to France with the British Expeditionary Force but he was captured in June 1940 when 51st Highland Division who were supporting the French Forces, were cut off from the coast and could not be evacuated back to England.

As a Prisoner of War of the German Army, he went through a succession of POW Camps but eventually made his escape from a POW Camp in what is now Poland in May 1942. Over the course of the next 9 months, he made his way across Europe evading capture until eventually he arrived in Spain. He was finally repatriated to England in April 1943.

The account of his escape demonstrated such extraordinary courage and resourcefulness that his chain of command almost immediately nominated him for a gallantry award. His Majesty King George VI signed the citation for the Military Medal and notice of the award was published in the *London Gazette* on 1st June 1943.

Interestingly the records in the Central Chancery in St James's Palace not only show the date of the announcement but also have a pencilled entry indicating that the presentation of the Military Medal by the King was scheduled for October 1943. However, his records then indicate that he was posted as absent without leave and in September 1943 they suggest that he had deserted. From a British Army point of view, nothing more was heard of him or from him. His medal record card kept by the Army Medal Office shows that the medal which had been struck and inscribed with his name was destroyed though there is no date.

Having established that he was never presented with his gallantry award nor was he ever charged or found guilty of any offence, there is the inevitable follow-up question as to whether he or his family should receive it now. Again, in short, the answer is yes and consequently, I have had a new contemporaneous Military Medal struck with his number, rank, name and Regiment inscribed on the rim. I have also looked at what other medals he may have been eligible to receive and it is clear from his records that he was eligible for the 1939–45 Star for his service in France and the War Medal 1939–45 for more than 28 days of war service. I have had new medals struck of both of these.

The final questions are for you to answer. The first is how you would wish to receive these three medals. I can either post them securely to you or if you wish, the British Defence Attaché has offered to host you and your family at the British Embassy in Dublin and formally present the medals to you. The last question is that currently I have each medal separate in its modern presentation box. I can have them swing mounted together as your father would have worn them on his uniform if you so wish or can leave them each in its box. The choice of how you would wish to receive the medals and if you would wish them mounted is yours and I would be grateful if you would let me know in due course.

I apologise again for the time taken to answer your simple question. There has been much discussion within the Army but we have undoubtedly arrived at the correct answer. I am only saddened that your father is not alive still to be honoured with his gallantry award – he was clearly a very courageous and resourceful man.

Yours sincerely,
Kestrel Simson

On 18 December 2018, my family and I were received by the British Ambassador and his wife and dignitaries at his residence in Dublin. Also in attendance was the international press. After a celebratory speech by the military attaché, Colonel Darren Doherty, my family was presented with the Military Medal, the 1939–45 Star, and the War Medal. I thanked the Colonel and His Excellency with a few words:

In my wildest dreams, I could not have imagined that I would be standing here today. It is a day that I and all my family will treasure for ever.

In the late afternoon of the 9th of March 1942, my father took the enormously brave decision to escape from Stalag XXA. He leapt into the woods and began his quest for freedom. In the Stalag, he left behind many companions whose friendship had been forged through extreme hardship. I imagine that when they heard of his escape, they let out a huge cheer to wish him luck. But that cheer was subdued somewhat by their knowing what would happen to him if he were caught. Today, in some place far beyond, those same men are hoisting Tom shoulder high and celebrating his achievement of which they are proud. However, they are not as proud as my family and I are.

Your Excellency, from the bottom of my heart, I want to sincerely thank you and the Army Medal Board for having the generosity of spirit of finally giving to my father the recognition of his courage and resilience that he so richly deserves, but never asked for when he was alive. Thank you.

The medals' ceremony in the British Ambassador's residence in Dublin.

My cousins were thrilled to hear of the award. Indeed, it brought a smile to my face when my cousin Rita, who lives in London, told me that her granddaughter Olivia's school had spent a morning discussing my dad's escape. Apparently, even his photos were put up all over the classroom!

Over the following weeks and months, I met with some elderly people from Waterford who had known my parents yet had never suspected what had really happened. They all agreed that being in the British Army, despite having been conscripted through no fault of his own, was not something you advertised in a small town in the south of Ireland in the 1950s or '60s. They all recounted that Tom and Lil were highly respected businesspeople in the city, well known for their generosity and their love of horse racing.

I do not know how Tom would have felt about the medals' award. He had no choice when it came to enlisting for war and we will never know what his thoughts were of his conscription. However, I do think that he would be very happy and relieved to know that a niggling cloud hanging over him for not returning to war after his escape had finally been lifted and his reputation vindicated. Also, I do know for sure that he would have been thoroughly chuffed to learn that his son and family cherish his memory with such love and affection. I can picture him now chuckling at the idea of being the leading character in a wartime memoir.

2. ORIGINAL NATIONAL ARCHIVES ESCAPE REPORT AND MILITARY RECORDS

The following is the original escape report that I retrieved on my visit to the National Archives in London. It laid the foundation for Part One of this book.

MOST SECRET

M.I.9/S/P.G.(Poland) 1189.

Escaped from STALAG XXA (3A) (THORN):
Evaded capture in FRANCE:
Interned in SPAIN.

The information contained in this report is to be treated as
MOST SECRET

ACCOUNT OF ESCAPE OF

T 117287 Cpl. M'GRATH, Thomas; R.A.S.C. Supply Section, 51 (H) Division.

Captured:	ST. VALERY-EN-CAUX, 11 Jun 40	Date of Birth:	17 Jan 04.
Escaped:	Stalag XXA (3A) (THORN, Poland) 9 Mar 42	Army Service:	Since 12 Oct 39.
Left:	GIBRALTAR, 25 Apr 43	Peacetime Profession:	Chauffeur - mechanic.
Arrived:	GOUROCK, 2 May 43	Private Address:	23 Kingscroft Road, LEATHERHEAD, Surrey.

1940
11 Jun
Captured
ST. VALERY-EN-CAUX

Sep or Oct
Stalag XXA (3A)
THORN (Poland)

I was captured on the beach at ST. VALERY-EN-CAUX on 11 Jun 40. After capture I was marched through Northern FRANCE and BELGIUM to HOLLAND, where after a train journey, we were put on barges and taken to GERMANY. I was for one or two nights in a transit camp at (?) HEMMER, and was then sent direct by train to the neighbourhood of THORN (Poland). At first (in Aug) I was in the "Balloon Hangar" one or two miles from THORN, and in Sep or Oct I was moved to Stalag XXA (3A) immediately South of the town of THORN.

I was not interrogated till about six months after my arrival in Stalag XXA (3A). All the Irishmen in the Camp were then interrogated. We were interrogated singly. I was interrogated by a tall man, aged about 37 or 38, who spoke good English. He had no trace of Irish accent, but had what might have been a German one. He asked me to sit down and gave me a cigarette. In reply to his first question, I said I was Irish, but lived in ENGLAND. He asked what I would do for the Irish cause in the case of trouble with ENGLAND, and I replied, as I had been advised to do by Sgt. Major STRAWBRIDGE, that I was a soldier and had no choice. The interrogator then spoke of what the English had done to IRELAND and how IRELAND would be free if GERMANY won the war. The interview lasted for about five minutes. I do not think the interrogator made any impression on any of the Irishmen then in the camp. Before that, however, about 20 or 30 Irishmen had been sent from Stalag XXA (3A) to BERLIN.

I prepared my escape from the camp for some time before I got away on 9 Mar 42. Cpl. CREAGAN, an Irishman who was in charge of a party working in the graveyard in THORN, managed to get me a suit of civilian clothes from a Polish woman, and I got a friend in ENGLAND
/to send me parcels ....

INTERVIEWED BY: I.S.9(W). 3 & 4 May 43;
M.I.5. 3 & 4 May; M.I.6(D). 4 May 43;
P.W.2(a). 4 May 43; D.A.G.(A), 5 May 43.

APPENDIX A - List of Helpers
Distribution: I.S.9. M.I.6(D).
I.S.9(W)

Distribution of this Report
D.D.M.I.(P/W) (2 copies). M.I.9. M.I.19.
I.S.9 (2 copies). I.S.9(W). M.I.9(d). M.I.6(D).
M.O.1 (S.P.) (Lt.-Col. Butters). Lt.-Col. Holt.
G.S."I", British Army Staff, Washington,
for POW Branch, MIS, War Dept (2 copies).
W/Cdr. F.W.Harrison (A.L.O., M.I.9).
M.I.9 Lecturers (5 copies).
S/Ldr. Evans (6 copies). Staff I.O., R.A.M.A.S.
File.

Retyped original escape report from the National Archives in London.

Escaped from Stalag XXA (3A) (THORN);
Evaded Capture in FRANCE;
Interned in SPAIN.

The information contained in this report is to be treated as MOST SECRET

ACCOUNT OF ESCAPE OF T 117287 Cpl. M'GRATH, Thomas; R.A.S.C. Supply Section, 51 (H) Division

Date of Birth: 17 Jan 04
Private Address: 23 Kingscroft Road, Leatherhead, Surrey.
Peacetime Profession: Chauffeur-mechanic
ARMY Service: Since 12 Oct 39
Captured: ST. VALERY-EN-CAUX, 11 Jun 40.
Escaped: Stalag XXA (3A) (THORN, Poland) 9 Mar 42
Left GIBRALTAR: 25 Apr 43
Arrived GOUROCK: 2 May 43

11 June 1940: Captured St-Valery-en-Caux
I was captured on the beach at St-Valery-en-Caux on 11 June 40.

After capture, I was marched through northern France and Belgium through Holland, where, after a train journey, we were put on barges and taken to Germany. I was for one or two nights in a transit camp at Hemer and was then sent direct by train to the neighbourhood of Thorn (Poland).

Sep or Oct Stalag XXA (3A) Thorn, Poland

At first (in Aug), I was in the 'Balloon Hangar', one or two miles from Thorn, and in Sept or Oct, I was moved to Stalag XXA (3A) immediately south of the town of Thorn.

I was not interrogated until about six months after my arrival in Stalag XXA (3A). All of the Irish men in the camp were then interrogated. We were interrogated singly. I was interrogated by a tall man, aged about 37 or 38, who spoke good English. He had no trace of [an] Irish accent, but had what might have been a German one. He asked me to sit down and gave me a cigarette. In reply to his first question, I said I was Irish, but lived in England. He asked what I would do for the Irish cause in the case of trouble with England, and I replied, as I had been advised to by Sgt Major Strawbridge, that I was a soldier and had no choice. The interrogator then spoke of what the English had done to Ireland and how Ireland would be free if Germany won the war. The interview lasted for about five minutes. I do not think the interrogator made any impression on any of the Irishmen then in the camp. Before that, however, about 20 or 30 Irishmen had been sent from Stalag XXA (3A) to Berlin.

I prepared my escape from the camp for some time before I got away on 9 Mar 42. Cpl. Creagan, an Irishman, who was in charge of a party working in the graveyard in Thorn, managed to get me a suit of civilian clothes from a Polish woman, and I got a friend in England to send me parcels containing underclothing, civilian shirts (which we were allowed to receive), socks and police boots. I exchanged the boots in the camp for a pair of civilian shoes. By raffling a silver cigarette case, I obtained about 200 marks in camp money which I exchanged for about 100 Reichsmarks. One of the men on a working party got me a map of Poland. I also collected a supply of chocolate and some soap.

From men who had made attempts to escape I gathered a certain amount of information on conditions outside. One man who had been recaptured in Danzig said that I might get a ship there, and eventually [I] decided to make for Danzig.

1942 9 Mar Escaped from Stalag XXA (3A)

On the afternoon of 9 Mar I went with the party which drew canteen supplies in the Kommandantur outside the main Stalag. Our German guard went to the Guard Room. While the rest of the party went for the supplies, I went first to a latrine and then, having satisfied myself there were no Germans about, I walked along a path which led to a back entrance of the camp. It was then, about 15:30 or 15:45 Hrs.

The Kommandantur was not wired. Had anyone called me, I would have said I was going back to the camp.

From the path, I got into a wood and hid in a hole dug by German soldiers who trained there. I was wearing civilian clothes under my uniform, and had with me a towel, soap, razor, chocolate, and tea. I stayed in the hole until it got dark and then walked east, north, and west, skirting the camp and also Fort 13. Eventually, after crossing some barbed wire, I came to a small house. I knocked at the door and an old Pole answered. After I had explained in German who I was, he took me in and put me into an attic. I showed him my map and indicated that I wanted to get to Danzig. He told me to stay in the attic. Before I reached the house I did not see or hear any sign of Germans searching for me. I had made no arrangements at the camp for my absence being covered up.

THORN

I stayed with the old man for three or four days, remaining in the attic all the time. One evening, the Pole gave me an old coat and cap and took me into Thorn. We crossed the river Vistula by the footpath on the railway bridge, passing a sentry who did not challenge us. In Thorn, the old Pole took me to the consulting room of a Polish oculist. The oculist, who spoke a little English, said he would help me, and that I would have to go to another house in Thorn until arrangements were made.

The old Pole then took me to a house, where I was sheltered by a Polish woman until June (about three months). During this time I did not go out at all.

At the beginning of June a Pole brought me 300 Reichsmarks, a suit of clothes and a 'working book' (a brown-covered book with a number of leaves in it. There was no photograph in the book). Next evening the Pole and I left Thorn together by train for Berlin. Before I left, the woman gave me a cloth handbag containing bread, a towel, and my shaving gear.

June: Berlin

We left Thorn about midnight and arrived to Berlin at the Schlerescherrabahnhof about 09:30 hrs next day. My papers were checked three or four times on the way. In the station my companion handed me over to another Pole who took me on foot to a slum in Berlin. I do not know the name of the district or the street. I stayed here from the beginning of June until the beginning of August. All this time I never went out, although my host often asked me to do so.

August: Left Berlin

At the beginning of August, my host brought me an identity card made out for a French man named Martin. He had a photograph of someone rather like me, and I had to part my hair to make the resemblance closer. The identity card was of the type issued to foreign workers in Germany. My host also gave me a yellow leaflet bearing the word 'Sonderzug' (special train) at the top. It bore three stamps and the name of a German firm. It had been issued to a French worker going home to Dijon on leave. I destroyed these documents in Miranda on the advice of Lieutenant Masson S/P.G. (F)1062.). I gave my host all the money I had, about 400 Reichsmarks, and he got me a ticket to Paris. That evening he took me to the Potsdamer Bahnhof where there was a crowd of 700 or 800 Frenchmen. I was introduced to a Frenchman with whom I was to travel and the Pole left. The train went out at 18:45 hrs.

Paris

We stopped at Hamm in the morning and got coffee. About noon, the train stopped at Herzogenrath, on the Dutch frontier. We had all to get out while the train was shunted to another platform and to rejoin the train we had to pass through a subway, where our tickets and identity cards were again checked. We then continued our journey to Paris via Maastricht and Namur. We reached Paris about 21:00 hrs on the 8 or 9 of August.

I left the train with the Frenchman with whom I had travelled. We waited until most of the people had left and then the Frenchman left me for a time, apparently looking for someone. While I was alone, a man approached me and asked if I was English. After he had spoken to the Frenchman, he told me to follow him and conducted me by underground to a flat in Sully-Morland. I gathered that my new helper, a Pole, had come to the station especially to meet me.

6 December Left Paris – St-Jean-de-Luz

I was sheltered in Paris from August until December, living with the Pole, partly in Sully-Morland and partly in Charlemagne. On 6 December I left Paris (Gare de l'Est[†]) with the Pole for St-Jean-de-Luz. I had no identity card and there was no control in the train. We left the station at St-Jean-de-Luz among a crowd of passengers and were not required to show identity cards there. My guide went into a café near the station and returned with a Basque, who gave me a beret and a pair of slippers. The Pole left me with the Basque.

The Basque guided me from St-Jean-de-Luz to the top of the Pyrenees, where he left me. I believe the guide was a smuggler. After leaving me, he went back to France.

Vera (Spain)

I continued down the mountains alone until I reached a road which I followed to a village. It was early morning and I sat down on the steps of a church. After about an hour and a half, a soldier or policeman came along and took me to his house. I discovered that the village was called Vera. After a visit to a superior official in another village, four or five km

† This is probably an error, and it is more likely the train left from Gare d'Austerlitz.

away, I was put in prison in Vera for two or three days. Here I was interrogated by a Spanish police officer, through an American woman acting as interpreter. He asked where I had come from and how I had crossed the Pyrenees.

10–16 December 1942 IRUN: 14 April 1943 Released from Miranda

I was moved to Irun about the 10th of December and imprisoned there until 16th of December. The British Consul in San Sebastian made arrangements for me to get food from outside. I was transferred to Miranda on the 16th of December and interned there until the 14th of April 1943. On my release I was in Madrid until the 22nd of April and was then sent to Gibraltar for repatriation, arriving on the 24th of April 1943.

Interviewed by:
I.S.9 (W). 3rd and 4th May 1943;
M.I.5., 3rd and 4th May 1943; M.I.6., 3rd and 4th May 1943;
P.W.2(s), 4th May 1943; D.A.G. 5th May 1943.

21.

IN MY PARENTS' FOOT-STEPS – FIVE JOURNEYS

Since discovering my father's military history, I have devoured books, articles and anything I could get my hands on relating to the BEF, the 51st Highland Division, the Maginot Line, the Battle of France, Rommel's capture of the 51st at Saint-Valery-en-Caux and, of course, Stalag XXA in Torun, Poland.

I felt I owed it to my father to visit the main sites where he had suffered such horrendous experiences. Similarly, having learned what my mother went through in her life, I felt I needed to also find out all I could about what she had endured.

I wanted to see what my parents had seen and try to imagine how they must have felt. I needed to feel their souls, to touch their hearts and get inside their heads. Most of all, I needed to get to know them better.

At the top of my list was to visit the Stalag in Torun, Poland. I wanted to go there while there was still a winter bite in the air in order to see if I could conjure up a sense, however minuscule, of what kind of suffering the POWs had to endure.

After that, I felt it would be rewarding to follow in my father's footsteps to cross the Pyrenees. I knew it would be impossible to get a sense of what he had actually gone through, but at least I would get a flavour of what it must have been like when he was there.

Next, I also wanted to visit the concentration camp at Miranda de Ebro. I often thought of how despondent and heartbreaking it must have been for my father, after almost a year hiding in shadows and finally escaping from Nazi-occupied territories, to have been thrown into a concentration camp in Spain, not knowing when, if ever, he would be liberated.

Map showing Tom's escape route across Europe.

I also cannot fathom what it must have been like for those men, having fought in bitter battles over many months, to hear the order to lay down their arms and surrender at

Saint-Valery-en-Caux. The desperation in their hearts must have been overwhelming. I wanted to go there to stand on the seashore, stare out at the horizon, and in my mind's eye see the fog descend that so cruelly quashed Tom's only hope of salvation.

In addition, having embarked on these voyages of discovery following in my father's steps, when I learned of my mother's experiences, I felt compelled to do the same for her, culminating in an emotional visit to Bessborough Mother and Baby Home.

JOURNEY 1:
STALAG XXA, FEBRUARY 2018

I visited Torun in mid-February 2018. It is a historical city situated on the River Vistula in the north-west of Poland. In the late nineteenth century the Prussian government started the construction of fortifications with the intention of building a ring of strongholds to surround the town. During the Second World War, some of the forts were used by the Germans as POW camps, one of which was known as Stalag XXA.

My guide, Pawel Bukowski, a giant of a man with a gentle and mannerly disposition, is a lecturer at a nearby university and also a tour guide with a passion for the history of the stalags in Torun.

The main gate at Stalag XXA during World War II.

It was freezing cold, and the biting wind went through to our bones. Bear in mind that here I was with my modern layered jacket and windbreaker. What must it have been like for those poor souls, war-worn, hungry and with hardly a stitch of clothing on their backs?

Torun has been the target of attack for centuries because of its location and changing borders. It has been invaded by, among others, Sweden, Prussia, Germany and the Soviet Union. Surprisingly, it has never been destroyed, although the Russians were about to do so during World War II when the German Army suddenly evacuated the city.

Me in front of the main entrance to the fort at Stalag XXA.

The main fort at Stalag XXA is now in a poor state and owned by a man who has no interest in maintaining it. In fact, he prohibits any access. In order to gain entry, my guide brought me across an adjacent forest and through a gap in the iron fencing. How ironic – I was now breaking into the very place my father had broken out of!

Inside the fort, even though it was daytime, we had to use torches for Pawel to show me the different chambers. We descended to the inner depths of the building where I was shown the confinement area– the 'cooler'– for POWs who were deemed to have misbehaved. For more serious offences, they were sent to labour camps to endure hard toil with restricted food rations. Greater offences, such as escape attempts, resulted in prisoners being shot.

The 'Cooler' at Stalag XXA.

*The cramped, muggy conditions that the POWs
were subjected to were atrocious.*

After visiting the fort, Pawel brought me to see the
bridge that Tom had crossed during his escape. The Vistula

is the widest and longest river in Poland, 1,047 km in length, running from the south to the north of Poland. On occasion the temperature can drop to minus 30 degrees. I have seen a photograph of cars driving across the water from one side to the other. While on the bridge, we were suddenly approached by two Polish policemen. It seems that now it is illegal for anyone to walk across it because of structural damage. As they began to shout at us, Pawel explained my father's story and they immediately said it was alright for us to be there.

Railway Bridge over River Vistula.

*Commemorative plaque beside the door
of the Resistance headquarters.*

On Saturday evening, Pawel walked with me around Torun. He showed me many insightful and interesting things that I would never have discovered on my own. One of these is the house that was the headquarters of the Resistance in Torun. Pawel was quite sure that at some stage Tom would have been brought here to be given false identity papers before travelling on to Berlin. (I touched the door!)

Pawel had recommended a good, modern hotel on the riverfront. When I went to book for this trip, however, that hotel was not available and I booked into a small hotel in the old part of town. While in this room, putting my thoughts together, I wrote the following:

The hotel is on a narrow street in the old part of town, just beside the market square. The room is no more than two and a half metres by one and a half metres. There is a small window behind the headboard that looks out on to a wall one metre in front. There is hardly anywhere to hang my clothes and the lighting is very poor. If I had a cat, I could not swing it. Tom was in Torun for months, pent up in a tiny attic. He didn't have central heating, a comfortable bed or an en suite toilet. Instead of feeling uncomfortable with my surroundings, I took the opportunity to savour the moment and to try and sense what it must have been like for Tom to have endured such a horrendous experience. Impossible! I knew that I could walk out that door at any time I wished. I knew where I was going to be in the coming days and weeks. I could sit down and enjoy a meal at my leisure. No one can know what he went through, and we never will.

It was not by chance that I had ended up in this room. Everything happens for a reason.

Even though most history books state that the stalags lasted from 1939 to 1945, in fact they continued to operate up to 1947. When the Germans invaded Poland in 1939, they arrested and imprisoned many of the locals. They imposed strict control and rules on Torun's population. Poles would have to show deference when crossing a German officer in the street or risk arrest. POWs from Britain, France, Australia and the Soviet Union began to arrive in 1940.

From 1944, the German guards changed their tone, became more lenient and, thanks to the Red Cross parcels, the men's physical condition vastly improved, which led to a boost in morale, so much so that they participated in sports and organised entertainment. There are also photographs of guards handing out cigarettes to smiling POWs. The Germans knew quite well what was coming and were doing their utmost to gain favour with their prospective captors.

Pawel also told me that once the Soviet Army arrived, things changed dramatically. When the Soviets eventually took over the camp in 1945, they treated the Russian POWs deplorably as had the Germans. They totally disregarded the Geneva Convention and subjected their fellow countrymen to brutal castigation. Food rations were limited so drastically that POWs from other countries would help by sharing food of their own. The Soviets imprisoned any captured Germans but eventually executed all remaining Russian POWs, putting into practice the propaganda slogan that the victims deserved it since real soldiers are never captured, and also the fact that Stalin did not want to see any soldier who had witnessed the ways of the West come back to contaminate the Motherland.

For the Polish people, life under communism, from 1945 to 1989, was far worse than anything that the country suffered under German occupation. Families were divided and no one trusted anyone.

On the Sunday morning, before heading to the airport, I went for a stroll around Torun. I called Eric in Melbourne and told him that I had spotted a webcam in the market square area where I was standing. He said that he would get on his computer to take a look. Little could Tom have imagined that, on the day before the fiftieth anniversary of his death, on 19 February 2018 (coincidentally also Asun's birthday), his son would be standing in that market square, speaking with his grandson who was also looking at the same square, but from the other side of the world!

Me waving to Eric in Melbourne via webcam from Torun's market square on the day before the fiftieth anniversary of Tom's death.

The following year, when speaking by phone with Pawel, he told me that a group of sons and daughters of POWs of Stalag XXA were planning a service to commemorate the seventy-fifth anniversary of the camp's liberation, to be held at the Stalag in May 2020. I subsequently made contact with the coordinator of the group and enthusiastically agreed to join them. Unfortunately, however, due to the Covid-19 pandemic it did not go ahead. I am hopeful that it will take place some day in the not-too-distant future.

JOURNEY 2:
CROSSING THE PYRENEES, JUNE 2018

The Hotel Saint Jacques is a small, pretty hotel situated on the fringe of the town of Saint-Jean-de-Luz in south-western France. On a bright June afternoon, my son Eric and I checked in at reception, having just got off the bus from Bilbao.

We took the elevator to the third floor and settled into our respective rooms. I walked over to my window, drew back the white curtains, and stood rooted to the floor at the sight of the Gare Saint-Jean-de-Luz dominating the view in front of me. This was the railway station where my father had arrived in December 1942, having escaped, alone, from Stalag XXA prisoner-of-war camp in Poland.

During my research, I had read that in 1940, a young woman from the Belgian Resistance, Andrée de Jongh, set up an escape network that came to be known as the 'Comet Line'. With the assistance of British Intelligence, MI6, the network helped Allied soldiers escape from Belgium and France to Spain and Gibraltar. After November 1942, the escape lines became more dangerous, when southern France was occupied by the Germans and the whole of France came under direct Nazi rule. Many members of the Comet Line were betrayed; hundreds were arrested and either executed or sent to concentration camps. It was not an easy route, as it was full of risk and danger, particularly during the winter months. German patrols were ever present, and the risk of encountering a wolf or bear was not unknown.

For those who managed to cross over the mountain, most made their way to San Sebastián and Bilbao, where they were assisted by the British Consulate.

Eric and I had come to Saint-Jean-de-Luz to follow in my father's footsteps over the Pyrenees into Spain, where he had hoped to find freedom. As it happens, we know the region extremely well because Asun was born in San Sebastián, less than half an hour's drive away.

I enjoyed showing Eric the train station at Saint-Jean-de-Luz, which I had passed through many times as a student to visit Asun, the same station Tom had arrived at before commencing his traverse of the Pyrenees. On his arrival in the town, Tom had been approached by a Basque smuggler who gave him a Basque beret and took him to the top of the Pyrenees before leaving him to walk down the other side to Spain on his own.

Early the following morning, we began our climb from a small town called Urrugne just outside Saint-Jean-de-Luz, my father's starting point. Back then, it was a narrow mountain track but nowadays the route to the top is a country road and, although the views were stunning, it was quite an incline, and we were glad to eventually reach the summit.

Eric and me at Saint-Jean-de-Luz Station.

Standing there amidst the many splendid peaks of this mighty mountain range, we were overcome by the thought of what it must have been like on that freezing December evening in 1942 when the surrounding forests were laden with terrible potential hidden dangers. We tried to imagine climbing up with someone who was being paid to show you part of the way – a *'contrabandista'*, smuggling escapers for cash – immersed in darkness and silence, while all around Europe was the violent turbulence of war. All that could be heard was the steady exhalation of breath growing faster as the incline progressed. Occasionally, between the tree branches, a sliver of light might have provided a shimmering glow from a wintry moon. My father might well have looked up to the stars and nodded in appreciation of all the guidance they had provided throughout his ordeal.

As Eric and I looked around, we could see that the scenery was spectacular, but Tom would likely not have been at all interested in the sights when he was there making his way down the side of the mountain, not knowing what lay ahead.

'Dad,' Eric said, 'we both speak Spanish. We know this region well and we know, more or less, what to expect when we get down to the other side. Your dad was alone, didn't speak the language and had no real idea of where he was going. Can you imagine how tiring and frightening it must have been to constantly look over your shoulder and watch out for German patrols or wild animals? The cold, the ice, the lack of appropriate clothing, the shrapnel wound on his leg and, worst of all, the emotional drain of not being able to mentally switch off. Always thinking of what ditch to jump into if needed, or what fields to cross without farmers noticing.'

Just then we heard the almighty roar of a heavy engine. While we both knew it was coming from a tractor of some sort, we looked at each other and quipped simultaneously: 'A tank!' This brought home a tiny fragment of what must have been going through my father's mind on those fateful days and nights.

*Looking out over the same Pyrenees mountain range
my father crossed during his escape.*

We reached the end of the mountain track, emerging in the town of Bera (also spelled Vera, depending on Spanish or Basque versions). And just as my father had described in his report, the first thing we saw were the steps of the church. This location has changed little since Tom was there.

The church in Bera town square.

We took a seat on those same steps and put our arms around each other. We knew that he was there with us. It was a moment we will treasure for ever.

Eric and me on the church steps in Bera, Spain.

JOURNEY 3:
MIRANDA DE EBRO, JULY 2019

A close friend from Málaga, Javier Herrera, expressed strong interest in my story when I told him about it one day. I mentioned to him that I was planning to visit the concentration camp in Miranda de Ebro, and he offered to join me. We did the necessary research of what a trip like this would entail and then met in Madrid and travelled to Miranda from there.

Javier and I met Carlos Diez, the curator of the new historical exhibition of the concentration camp, which had been inaugurated only a few months previously. Carlos brought us to the local civic centre where the exhibition is housed in a basement. I had been expecting to see a re-creation of parts of the camp, but what we found was a clinical layout of photographs, videos, personal possessions and a constructed copy of a hut in which the prisoners had slept. I have read a lot about what the prisoners there had to endure at the camp and, to me, the exhibition did not accurately portray the true horrors that prevailed there at the time.

During my visit to the Stalag in Poland, I felt an immediate connection – I became part of the place for the short time I was there. Here, however, it was as if I had stepped into a schoolroom to attend a class on the subject. This is a pity because there are remnants of the building remaining on the original site of the camp.

Holding a photo of my father at Miranda de Ebro concentration camp. (Courtesy of Javier Herrera)

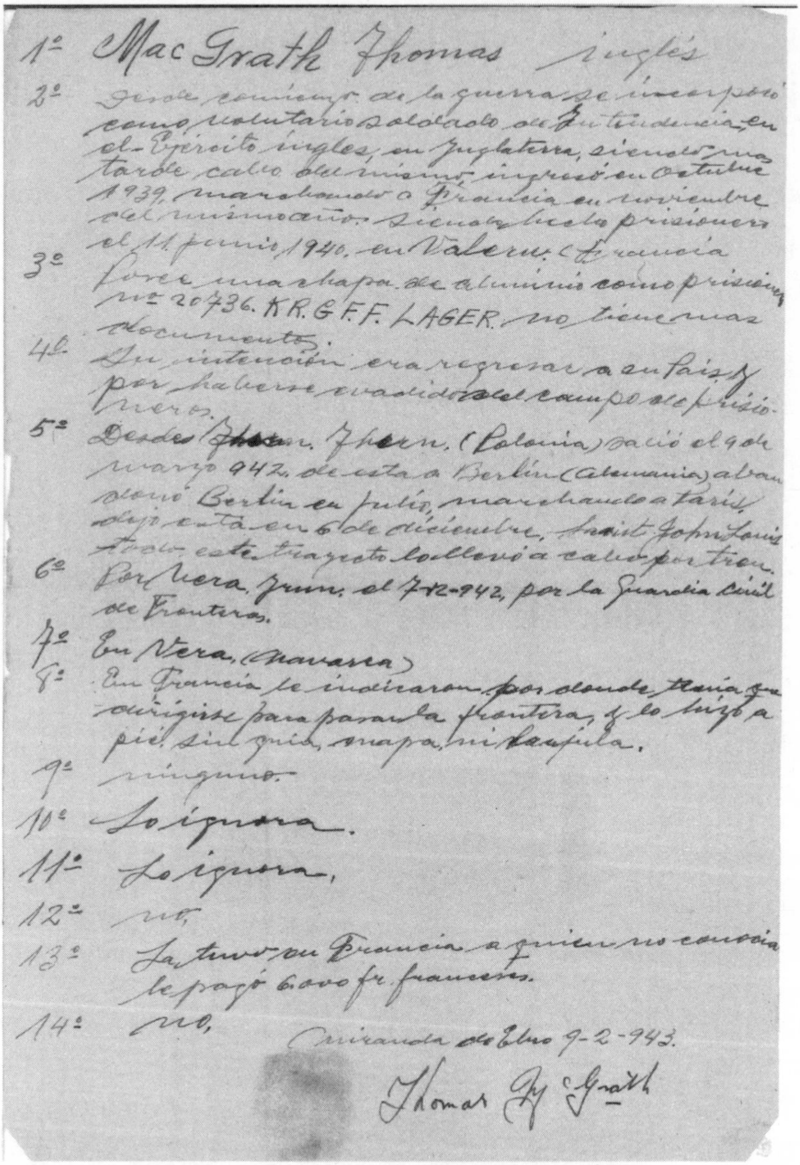

1º MacGrath Thomas inglés

2º *[handwritten Spanish text]*

3º *[handwritten Spanish text]* nº 20736. K.R.G.F.F. LAGER. *[handwritten Spanish text]*

4º *[handwritten Spanish text]*

5º *[handwritten Spanish text]*

6º *[handwritten Spanish text]*

7º En Vera. (Navarra)

8º *[handwritten Spanish text]*

9º ninguno.

10º Lo ignora.

11º Lo ignora.

12º no.

13º *[handwritten Spanish text]*

14º no.

Miranda de Ebro 9-2-943.

Thomas Mc Grath

Copy of original replies to questions put to Tom on his arrival at Miranda. It is interesting to see that he refuses to answer requests for information about who had assisted him in his escape.

JOURNEY 4:
SAINT-VALERY-EN-CAUX, NOVEMBER 2019

Field Marshal Erwin Rommel stands beside Major General Fortune, having captured over 11,000 French and British soldiers after three days' fierce battle in Saint-Valery-en-Caux on 12 June 1940.

Eric and me at the same spot in November 2019.

In November 2019, Eric and I travelled to the northern French port town of Saint-Valery-en-Caux, where my father and the rest of the 51st Highland Division had been captured many years before.

Having driven through narrow country roads in freezing, snowy conditions, we checked into our hotel and immediately set about finding somewhere to eat. All we could find open at that time of night was a small take-away pizza bar. This met our needs splendidly. I could not stop thinking of the unfairness of life when comparing this simple indulgence with what had occurred in the same surroundings nearly eighty years before.

Later, as we walked around the narrow streets, we tried to imagine what it must have been like for the French or British soldiers who had fought their way to this small coastal town on retreat in the hope of being rescued by the navy. What enemy waited around every corner of these narrow streets? How did these men feel as they engaged in fierce hand-to-hand combat, knowing full well that to survive they had to come out on top?

As we walked back to the square and our hotel, we tried to envisage the mounds of bodies piled high during those horrific days while the wounded lay strewn all around. Their cries of pain still reverberate through the narrow streets of this quaint town, which had over seventy per cent of its buildings destroyed in the fighting.

The navy came, but, owing to bad weather, fog, and the pounding of artillery from the panzer tanks encircling the town on the cliffs above, only a handful of men managed to actually get away. Others tried to flee to safety by using makeshift ropes or belts tied together to scale down the jagged cliffs. Many fell in doing so and perished on the rocks below, while others became easy targets for the German snipers to pick off. There were also those who, in their desperation, chose to jump to their deaths.

Eric and me at the cliffs at St-Valery-en-Caux.

It is hard to imagine the condition that the men found themselves in at this stage, after fighting battle after battle against the invading force. By the time they reached the beach, food and ammunition had long run out. Now their only hope was the navy. Tantalisingly, they could see their rescue ships through fog on the horizon, but as the hours passed and dusk turned to dawn, word filtered down that the order had been given to lay down arms. How frustrating it must have been for the troops to receive this news. They were within touching distance of safety; British shores were only twenty miles across the English Channel. But everyone must have felt so hopeless, surrendering to the Germans, not knowing what torture would lie ahead.

Each year, Saint-Valery-en-Caux commemorates the battle that was fought in 1940. In 2010, to celebrate the seventieth anniversary, veterans from France, Britain, and other countries gathered there to remember the sacrifices that had been made and to give thanks for the legacy of peace for which they had laid the foundation.

A memorial to the bravery of the 51st Highland Division has been erected on the clifftop.

JOURNEY 5:
BESSBOROUGH, JUNE 2021

In June 2021, Asun and I travelled to Cork to visit our daughter Cristina and her family. Since discovering my mother's heart-breaking story, it had always been at the back of my mind that I should go and see what Bessborough House looked like and perhaps get more of a feeling of what she had gone through all those years ago. I mentioned it to Ken, Cristina's husband, and he immediately volunteered to bring me and show me where the building was. On the way, I told him that I had also discovered that I was born in a nursing home in Cork called Glenvera and he very kindly made a detour so that we could pass by this location also.

When we arrived, I looked up at the building, which has the name 'Glenvera' signposted on the front. It was obvious that, in its day, it had been an impressive building right in the heart of the city. Nowadays, it is run as a refuge for asylum seekers; however, when Lil went there for my birth, it was a private nursing home which, I understand, was quite exclusive at the time.

After our brief stop at Glenvera, we continued on our journey until we came to a sign saying 'Sacred Heart Convent'. The gate was open to an entrance that led to a long driveway with overhanging trees on one side and extensive green fields on the other. I had been expecting the entrance to be closed, or at least show a 'no entry' sign. There were no such signs.

As I sat in the passenger seat in silence, my mind began to try to imagine what it must have been like for my poor mother, as a young girl, travelling along the same road, not sure of what lay before her. Feeling so alone, she must have been absolutely terrified.

At the end of the driveway, we turned a bend to find ourselves in a forecourt dominated by a large three-storey Georgian mansion. Five stone steps, flanked by two stone lion ornaments on plinths, led up to an enormous entrance.

I climbed the steps and put my hand on the wooden door. I closed my eyes to imagine being brought back to that moment on Saint Patrick's Day in 1939. I imagined celebrations must have been in full flow all over the city. I visualised a hooded nun slowly opening the door, her face hidden in the dim light, and ushering me in to the dark hallway. I could sense my mother's trembling presence and hear her suppressed sobbing. I looked around in the darkness of my mind to find her and comfort her, but when I opened my eyes, she was no longer there.

The feelings of outrage and injustice burned deep within me as I clasped two photos I had brought with me; one of Lil, my mother, and the other of her son, Cyril-Patrick, my half-brother. I stared at them and said to myself, *What was done to you both was cruel and unforgivable. You lived in different days when backward prejudices, religious terror, and stigma, deprived you of the right and joy to know and love one another. Thankfully, you both had the courage to go on and make the most of your lives and bring happiness and love to others. I am so very happy and fortunate that I have discovered all that I have in the past few years.*

I left the grounds with the feeling that I had accomplished something that had to be done. I know that Lil in her wildest dreams could never have imagined that one day I would visit the place she never spoke about, nor have found the son who was taken cruelly from her and whom she never got to meet. I know that she would be overjoyed that I did.

In front of Bessborough Mother and Baby Home, Cork.
I am holding photographs of my mother and half-brother.

———

Was it worth my while to have gone to visit Torun and the Stalag? To climb with Eric over the Pyrenees and take time to see what was left of the concentration camp in Miranda? To stand on the beach in Saint-Valery-en-Caux and imagine the panzer guns pointing down from the cliffs, knowing that all was lost? And was it worth my visit to Bessborough, to stand at the door through which my mother had walked?

Without question, it was.

These trips have afforded me the opportunity to peek through the window of time and achieve some clarity regarding what it must have been like in those dreadful days.

For my father to have escaped a POW camp and to have returned home across an occupied Europe was no mean feat. I knew he was a man full of tenderness and affection, but his journey also proved that he possessed a determination of steel and an unrelenting will to live. I can only assume that my parents must have identified these shared traits in each other, since my mother's suffering in the twisted social norms of the time would also have been enough to derail anybody. Instead, she paved a way for herself, holding her head high. She created a thriving business and started her own family during those suffocating times, while all the while longing for the baby who had been taken away from her.

It made me feel proud to follow in their footsteps, to retrace the paths they had travelled, which moulded their lives and indeed their personalities and outlook. It was valuable to me, in terms of connection and closure, to undertake these journeys into the past. It has provided me with a unique opportunity to get to know my parents better than when they were alive. It has also introduced them to my children and has allowed them to cherish and appreciate the wonderful people their grandparents were and achieve an awareness of what those of that generation went through in their lives.

EPILOGUE:
BREAKING THE SILENCE

One night, when I was very small, perhaps six or seven, I could not sleep. Tom took me into the living room and let me play with my toys on the floor. He sat and read the paper with a cigarette and a glass of whiskey. I have a vague memory of him telling me about different countries and, in particular, Poland and Spain. I do not recall any reference to the war or a POW camp. On that, he remained silent.

Another evening, I watched my mother tending to my father's leg. The cold, wet cloth she tied firmly around his thigh must have helped. The first time I saw her doing it, I was probably about five. I had been frightened to see his face contort in pain. There was no bleeding or cut that I could see. I was puzzled as to what had happened. When I asked, Aunt Lil simply said that he had fallen a long time ago and hurt his leg.

These were the small silences and confusions that existed throughout my childhood but of which I had no sense back then. I was unaware of it, but every time I uttered the words 'Uncle Tom' and 'Aunt Lil', I was falling into another of those silences, another absence forced on my parents by the world they lived in. It has taken me a long, long time to discover my family background and fill in the gaps that were there for so long.

Both Tom and Lil kept their own secrets for different reasons, and these untold stories would have lain hidden for ever were it not for the fortuitous twists and turns of life. For that, I will always be grateful. Thanks to the discovery of my cousins on my father's side, I unearthed my father's story. And thanks to my father's story attracting attention, my cousin on my mother's side found me – and broke the news about the half-brother I never knew existed. Writing this account has been a journey back in time to a happy but incomplete childhood. At last, I can clear the opacity that was always there, buried in my subconscious. I find it an intriguing coincidence that my mother endured the horrific experience of her child being taken from her in 1939, the very same year that my father was conscripted into the British Army. Their lives had not yet intertwined, yet they suffered unspeakable hardships in parallel.

Now, after so many decades have passed, I can look back and realise that there is a common theme connecting me to my parents. Something all three of us shared is that we never spoke of the past. My father, for not wanting to relive the horrors he had suffered and for fear of retribution from British authorities or threats closer to home. My mother, out of social prejudice, pressure and its accompanying shame. And me, from a subconscious fear of the stigma of being different.

When I fell in love with Asun, I felt I had to tell her about my unusual childhood. It took me a huge effort to do so, and I still recall how very nervous I was when recounting my story. It was as though I was afraid of an adverse reaction, that I would lose her. But she understood, and it brought us even closer.

Both my children were adults when I eventually told them what little information I knew about my past, in what for me was a highly emotional moment. They understood and loved me for sharing part of their heritage with them.

I feel very privileged and lucky to have made these life-changing discoveries. At the beginning, to get a complete picture of what had happened all those years ago, a strong determination and a lot of hard work was required, beginning with research in the National Archives in Kew, which resulted in visits to important locations, background studies and interviews. I also needed time and bucketloads of passion. Armed with this, I decided that in writing the book I would stay faithful to the National Archives' account. I would use the names of people and places referred to in the account, and I would try to find the names of people and places not directly mentioned in the account. For instance, the Commander of Stalag XXA at the time was in fact Hauptmann Schubert, Samuel Hoare was the British ambassador in Madrid, and the embassy was located on Fernando El Santo Street.

In the fast world that we live in, where everything is instant, it is easy to forget those who have gone before us. Writing this book has taught me the importance of slowing down to remember the people of my parents' generation, many of whom were subjected to terrible physical and mental torment at the hands of tyrants while others passively looked on. At times, I feel a sense of guilt when I look back at my life of comfort in comparison to what many of my parents' generation went through. When I think of the enormous injustice that was thrust upon them, I am overcome with outrage. I hope that the stories in this book will help them never to be forgotten.

After reading so many books on the Battle of France and life in the Stalags, and learning about the atrocities committed and the level of depravity that some stooped to, I sometimes ask myself if there is any hope for mankind. War brings out the worst in people. However, it can also bring out the best. For example, one act of selfless generosity was carried out by that old Polish man who opened the door to my father and hid him in his attic, putting his own life at risk in doing so. It could have all ended so differently, were it not for moments like this, in which altruistic and noble gestures and deeds prevailed against the odds.

Days before finishing this book, my daughter gave birth to her first child. Cristina and her husband, Ken, called their new-born baby Lily, after my mother. This was so touching for me, and it shows the enormous effect that all these revelations have had on my family.

This account is for my family, my children Eric and Cristina, and for my grandchildren Luca, Lily, Mila, Jack and those yet to follow. Let them never forget their forefathers. They too were real people who worked hard, laughed, played, cried and dreamed of a better future for their children.

When I was a small boy, I was wrapped in love and adoration. After all that he had been through, my father probably never imagined in his wildest dreams that one day he would have a son. He was a gentleman with a heart of gold who kept his wartime past to himself. Tom would often say, 'Never be afraid to take a chance.' It is only now that I understand what he meant.

And my poor mother, after what she had endured, held on to me tightly and refused to let me go, as had so cruelly happened to her before. Lil was a quiet, generous and warm lady. Knowing what I now know, her inner suffering must have been with her always and I admire her greatly for creating a happy life for us in spite of that.

My parents used to remind me jokingly that they would one day be gone. The thought terrified me. So much so that I would go on my knees beside my bed every night when I was a little boy and say this prayer:

As I lay on my bed to sleep, I pray to God my soul to keep.
And if I die before I wake, I pray to God my soul to take.
God bless all and please don't take Tom or Lil for a long
  time yet!

I loved them dearly and miss them terribly.

Lil and Tom, my parents.

May they rest in peace.

ACKNOWLEDGEMENTS

A most important thanks should go to my daughter, Cristina, who has been a strong driving force for this book right from the very start. Since her early teenage years she has consistently encouraged me to do everything possible to find out more about her Irish heritage. It was in her initial research that she made the important early discoveries, from which the full story emerged, resulting in this book. I owe her a great deal of gratitude for her enormous emotional interest in unearthing our family's history and continued determination to leave no stone unturned to do so. Thank you, Cristina; I love you dearly, and I am very grateful for your endless support.

Thank you also to Ken, Cristina's husband, and his father, John Hogan, for finding John Aylward. Unbeknownst to anyone at the time, John Aylward turned out to be crucial in laying the first stone in the foundation of this story by introducing me to my unknown McGrath cousins. Without that, none of this would have come to light. Thank you, John Aylward, it has been quite a journey since that day we met!

And what cousins they turned out to be! I feel blessed and fortunate that they have come into my life and my family's life at this stage of my life. We have become very close and share a unique bond of friendship.

My deepest gratitude also goes out to my cousin Denis Vaughan. Had he not reached out to me when the story was revealed, I would never have known of other extraordinary revelations that have changed my life. These revelations led to me finding new loved ones whom I value dearly. It was a brave step, Denis, for which I will be forever grateful.

I also want to thank my nieces, Angela and Marie, and their families, for the warmth and love that they have given to my family. It has added so much to our lives.

I must also acknowledge the patience and support of my wife, Asun, as this became a project that has overtaken and changed my life. She was most supportive and enthusiastic from the outset, as well as throughout the entire journey of discoveries and endless hours of writing. She welcomed with open arms all new family members and undertook on her own the tremendous work of compiling and drafting a most detailed family tree. It was outstanding and much appreciated by all, as it provided great clarity when wading through reams of unfamiliar information. When we met as teenagers I was an only child with no parents and no brothers or sisters – someone with a vague notion of maybe having a few cousins somewhere in the world. She and her family took a leap of faith and embraced me for who I was. Her parents blindly took me under their wing and exerted a strong influence on me, guiding me with love and support in important life-changing decisions. For that unconditional acceptance I am eternally grateful.

I wish to thank my dear friend Ita Daly, who was one of the first people I told of my discovery. Her advice and support have been invaluable. It was Ita who first mooted the idea of having the book published because she fervently believed that there would be public interest in a story that highlights not only the atrocities of war, but also exposes the cruelty of society in Ireland at that time in history. I am deeply grateful to her for her support and encouragement and, most of all, for her belief in me.

I have always been an avid reader of war-related matters. One book that I read shortly before learning about my father's story was Bob Jackson's wonderful *A Doctor's Sword*. Upon discovering my dad's escape story, I sought out Bob, and he kindly agreed to meet me. At the time, I was toying with the idea of looking for an author who might be interested in writing a book about my story. After I relayed to him the background of my discovery, Bob said that the escape account was fascinating but the context and background provided an opportunity to tell a broader story about human courage in the face of adversity and also to shine a torch on the suffering that the protagonists endured. He encouraged me to write the story myself, and for this I am deeply grateful.

I would also like to say a special word of thanks to genealogist, Paul Gorry, who has been so valuable in helping me find out more about my family. My constant phone calls, emails, and texts were always met with a smile.

I want to thank my good friend Nicky Fitzpatrick for his guidance and support in pointing me in the right direction when dealing with the British Army authorities.

I would like to extend a huge 'thank you' my dear friend Javier Herrera for accompanying me on the fact-finding trip to the Miranda de Ebro concentration camp. From the beginning he has shown huge support and a keen interest in all my updates as they came through. In particular, I want to thank him for composing and dedicating a most touching poem to me on my journey to discover my family's past. I value his friendship dearly.

I am also very grateful to Djinn von Noorden for her invaluable help in the early stages of copyediting the manuscript.

My most heartfelt thanks to Jonathan Williams. Never in my wildest dreams did I think that I would have my own literary agent! Jonathan has a rare talent in that he extracts the very best from you by exuding enthusiasm, wisdom and encouragement to strive for perfection. I have never met anyone with such attention to detail. I would present him with a revised manuscript, he would sprinkle some of his magic dust over it and – hey presto! – suddenly all the errors of grammar were eliminated and the story put into proper context. To crown it all, he does so in such a gentle and courteous manner.

I wish to express my sincere thanks to Jonathan for his interest in my family story, and I greatly appreciate the advice that he has given and the time that he has spent highlighting areas for improvement.

It has been to my tremendous good fortune that Gill Books decided to take my work and have it published. The team assigned to it have been so refreshingly helpful and professional that it has been a joy and a pleasure to work closely with them. I am immensely grateful to all, especially Nicki, Sarah, Aoibheann, Laura, Teresa and Fiona. Thank you for making it happen.

I am very grateful to Rachel Pierce for all her helpful advice in editing the book. She skilfully guided me to enhance sections of the story that would have lain bare without her input. As a result, the story benefited immensely. Any errors or inaccuracies contained in the book are entirely mine and mine alone.

My final thanks are reserved for my parents. Through the writing of this book I feel that I have got to know them better than when they were alive. It is to them that I owe the greatest thanks of all.

I was never afforded the opportunity to thank them in person for their bravery in keeping me in the face of the harsh circumstances and social prejudices they had to endure.

In the few brief years we had together, they gave me enough love to last a lifetime. They instilled in me the values of having a moral compass, compassion and resilience. For this, I am deeply indebted to them. These are qualities that I value greatly and can also see in my children, and will, I hope, be inherited by their own children, my grandchildren. After all, it is for them that this book was written. One day, they can read this book to peel back the curtain of time and catch a glimpse of a bygone era that helped in the formation of who they are.

The McGrath family.